INTERACTIVE WHITEBOARD ACTIVITIES

Grades 2–3

Math

LESSONS FOR THE SMART BOARD™

Motivating, Interactive Lessons That Teach Key Math Skills

■SCHOLASTIC

New York ○ Toronto ○ London ○ Auckland ○ Sydney
New Delhi ○ Mexico City ○ Hong Kong ○ Buenos Aires

Teaching Resources

Author: Ann Montague-Smith
Illustrators: Jim Peacock, Jenny Tulip, Theresa Tibbetts
Editor: Maria L. Chang
Cover design: Brian LaRossa
Interior design: Grafica Inc.

CD-ROM developed in association with Q & D Multimedia.

Special thanks to Robin Hunt and Melissa Rugless of Scholastic Ltd.

SMART Board™ and Notebook™ are registered trademarks of SMART Technologies Inc.
Microsoft Office, Word, and Excel are either registered trademarks or trademarks of Microsoft Corporation in the United States and/or other countries.

All Flash activities designed and developed by Q & D Multimedia.

Interactive Teaching Programs (developed by the Primary National Strategy) © Crown copyright.

Contents

Introduction

Interactive whiteboards are fast becoming the must-have resource in today's classroom as they allow teachers to facilitate children's learning in ways that were inconceivable a few years ago. The appropriate use of interactive whiteboards, whether used daily in the classroom or once a week in a computer lab, encourages active participation in lessons and increases students' determination to succeed. Interactive whiteboards make it easier for teachers to bring subjects across the curriculum to life in new and exciting ways.

What can an interactive whiteboard offer?

For teachers, an interactive whiteboard allows them to do the same things they can on an ordinary whiteboard, such as drawing, writing, and erasing. However, the interactive whiteboard also offers many other possibilities, such as:

- saving any work created during a lesson;
- preparing as many pages as necessary;
- displaying any page within the Notebook™ file to review teaching and learning;
- adding scanned examples of children's work to a Notebook file;
- changing colors of shapes and backgrounds instantly;
- using simple templates and grids;
- linking Notebook files to spreadsheets, Web sites, and presentations.

Using an interactive whiteboard in the simple ways outlined above can enrich teaching and learning in a classroom, but that is only the beginning of the whiteboard's potential to educate and inspire.

For students, the interactive whiteboard provides the opportunity to share learning experiences, as lessons can be delivered with sound, still and moving images, and Web sites. Interactive whiteboards can be used to cater to the needs of all learning styles:

- Kinesthetic learners benefit from being able to physically manipulate images.
- Visual learners benefit from being able to watch videos, look at photographs, and see images being manipulated.
- Auditory learners benefit from being able to access audio resources, such as voice recordings and sound effects.

With a little preparation, all of these resource types could be integrated into one lesson—a feat that would have been almost impossible before the advent of the interactive whiteboard!

Access to an interactive whiteboard

In schools where students have limited access to an interactive whiteboard, carefully planned lessons will help students get the most benefit from it during the times they can use it. As teachers become familiar with the interactive whiteboard, they will learn when to use it and, equally important, when not to use it!

Where permanent access to an interactive whiteboard is available, it is important to plan the use of the board effectively. It should be used only in ways that will enhance or extend teaching and learning. Children still need to gain practical, firsthand experience of many things. Some experiences cannot be recreated on an interactive whiteboard, but others cannot be had without it. *Math Lessons for the SMART Board*™ offers both teachers and learners the most accessible and creative uses of this most valuable resource.

About the book

Adapted from Scholastic UK's best-selling 100 SMART Board™ Lessons series, *Math Lessons for the SMART Board*™ is designed to reflect best practice in using interactive whiteboards. It is also designed to support all teachers in using this valuable tool by providing lessons and other resources that can be used on the SMART Board with little or no preparation. These inspirational lessons meet the Common Core State Standards for Mathematics and the National Council of Teachers of Math (NCTM) standards and are perfect for all levels of experience.

This book is divided into four chapters. Each chapter contains lessons covering:

- Number & Operations
- Algebra Readiness
- Measurement & Data Analysis
- Geometry

Mini-Lessons

The mini-lessons have a consistent structure that includes:

- a **Getting Started** activity;
- a step-by-step **Mini-Lesson** plan;
- an **Independent Work** activity; and
- a **Wrap-Up** activity to round up the teaching and learning and identify any assessment opportunities.

Each mini-lesson identifies any resources required (including Notebook files that are provided on the CD-ROM, as well as reproducible activity pages) and lists the whiteboard tools that could be used in the mini-lesson.

The reproducible activity sheets toward the back of the book support the mini-lessons. These sheets provide opportunities for group or individual work to be completed away from the board, while linking to the context of the whiteboard lesson. They also provide opportunities for whole-class discussions in which children present their work.

What's on the CD-ROM?

The accompanying CD-ROM provides an extensive bank of Notebook files designed for use with the SMART Board. These support, and are supported by, the mini-lessons in this book. They can be annotated and saved for reference or for use with subsequent lessons; they can also be printed out. In addition to texts and images, a selection of Notebook files include the following types of files:

- **Embedded Microsoft PowerPoint and Excel files:** The embedded files are launched from the Notebook file and will open in their native Microsoft application.
- **Embedded interactive files:** These include specially commissioned interactive files that will open in a new browser window within the Notebook environment.
- **Embedded audio files:** Some Notebook files contain buttons that play sounds.
- **"Build Your Own" file:** This contains a blank Notebook page with a bank of selected images and interactive tools from the Gallery, as well as specially commissioned images. You can use this to help build your own Notebook files.

The Notebook files

All of the Notebook files have a consistent structure as follows:

- **Title and objectives page**—Use this page to highlight the focus of the mini-lesson. You might also wish to refer to this page at certain times throughout the lesson or at the end of the lesson to assess whether the learning objective was achieved.
- **Getting Started activity**—This sets the context of the lesson and usually provides some key questions or learning points that will be addressed through the main activities.
- **Main activities**—These activities offer independent, collaborative group, or whole-class work. The activities draw on the full scope of Notebook software and the associated tools, as well as on the SMART Board tools. "What to Do" boxes are also included in many of the prepared Notebook files. These appear as tabs in the top right-hand corner of the screen. To access these notes, simply pull out the tabs to reveal planning information, additional support, and key learning points.
- **Wrap-Up**—A whole-class activity or summary page is designed to review work done both at the board and away from the board. In many lessons, children are encouraged to present their work.

How to Use the CD-ROM

Setting up your screen for optimal use

It is best to view the Notebook pages at a screen display setting of 1280 x 1024 pixels. To alter the screen display, select Settings, then Control Panel from the Start menu. Next, double-click on the Display icon, then click on the Settings tab. Finally, adjust the Screen Area scroll bar to 1280 x 1024 pixels. Click on OK. (On the Mac, click on the apple icon and select System Preferences. Then click on Displays and select 1280 x 1024.)

If you prefer to use a screen display setting of 800 x 600 pixels, ensure that your Notebook view is set to "Page Width." To alter the view, launch Notebook and click on View. Go to Zoom and select the "Page Width" setting. If you use a screen display setting of 800 x 600 pixels, text in the prepared Notebook files may appear larger when you edit it on screen.

Getting started

The program should run automatically when you insert the CD-ROM into your CD drive. If it does not, use My Computer to browse to the contents of the CD-ROM and click on the Scholastic icon. (On the Mac, click on the Scholastic icon to start the program.)

Main menu

The Main menu divides the Notebook files by topic: Number & Operations; Algebra Readiness; Measurement & Data Analysis; and Geometry. Clicking on the appropriate button for any of these options will take you to a separate Lessons menu. (See below for further information.) The "Build Your Own" file is also accessed through the Main menu.

Individual Notebook files or pages can be located using the search facility by keying in words (or part of words) from the resource titles in the Search box. Press Go to begin the search. This will bring up a list of the titles that match your search.

Lessons menu

Each Lessons menu provides all of the prepared Notebook files for each chapter of the book. Click on the buttons to open the Notebook files. Click on Main menu button to return to the Main menu screen. (To alternate between the menus on the CD-ROM and other open applications, hold down the Alt key and press the Tab key to switch to the desired application.)

"Build Your Own" file

Click on this button to open a blank Notebook page and a collection of Gallery objects, which will be saved automatically into the My Content folder in the Gallery. (Under My Content, open the Year 3 Folder, then the Math folder to access the Gallery objects.) You only need to click on this button the first time you wish to access the "Build Your Own" file, as the Gallery objects will remain in the My Content folder on the computer on which the file was opened. To use the facility again, simply open a blank Notebook page and access the images and interactive resources from the same folder under My Content. If you are using the CD-ROM on a different computer, you will need to click on the "Build Your Own" button again.

Safety note: Avoid looking directly at the projector beam as it is potentially damaging to the eyes, and never leave children unsupervised when using the interactive whiteboard.

Connections to the Math Standards

The mini-lessons and activities in this book meet the following Common Core State Standards for Mathematics and the National Council of Teachers of Mathematics (NCTM) Standards:

	COMMON CORE STATE STANDARDS	NCTM STANDARDS
NUMBER & OPERATIONS		
Counting in Tens and Ones	**2.NBT.2:** Count within 1000; skip-count by 5s, 10s, and 100s. **3.OA.9:** Identify arithmetic patterns (including patterns in the addition table), and explain them using properties of operations.	• Use multiple models to develop initial understandings of place value and the base-ten system. • Describe, extend, and make generalizations about geometric and numeric patterns.
Expanding Numbers	**2.NBT.3:** Read and write numbers to 1000 using base-ten numerals, number names, and expanded form. **2.NBT.5:** Fluently add and subtract within 100 using strategies based on place value. **2.NBT.9:** Explain why addition and subtraction strategies work, using place value and the properties of operations. **3.NBT.2:** Fluently add and subtract within 1000 using strategies and algorithms based on place value.	• Use multiple models to develop initial understandings of place value and the base-ten system. • Understand the effects of adding and subtracting whole numbers. • Develop and use strategies for whole-number computations, with a focus on addition and subtraction. • Recognize equivalent representations for the same number and generate them by decomposing and composing numbers.
Ordering Numbers	**2.NBT.1:** Understand that the three digits of a three-digit number represent amounts of hundreds, tens, and ones. **2.NBT.4:** Compare two three-digit numbers based on meanings of the hundreds, tens, and ones digits.	• Develop understanding of the relative position and magnitude of whole numbers and of ordinal and cardinal numbers and their connections. • Understand the place-value structure of the base-ten number system and be able to represent and compare whole numbers and decimals.
Hundreds, Tens, and Ones	**2.NBT.1:** Understand that the three digits of a three-digit number represent amounts of hundreds, tens, and ones.	• Use multiple models to develop initial understandings of place value and the base-ten system. • Recognize equivalent representations for the same number and generate them by decomposing and composing numbers. • Understand the place-value structure of the base-ten number system and be able to represent and compare whole numbers and decimals.
Base-10 Numbers	**2.NBT.1:** Understand that the three digits of a three-digit number represent amounts of hundreds, tens, and ones. **2.NBT.3:** Read and write numbers to 1000 using base-ten numerals, number names, and expanded form.	• Use multiple models to develop initial understandings of place value and the base-ten system. • Recognize equivalent representations for the same number and generate them by decomposing and composing numbers. • Understand the place-value structure of the base-ten number system and be able to represent and compare whole numbers and decimals.
Number Facts	**2.OA.2:** Fluently add and subtract within 20 using mental strategies.	• Understand various meanings of addition and subtraction of whole numbers and the relationship between the two operations. • Understand the effects of adding and subtracting whole numbers. • Develop and use strategies for whole-number computations, with a focus on addition and subtraction. • Develop fluency with basic number combinations for addition and subtraction.
Inverse Operations	**2.OA.2:** Fluently add and subtract within 20 using mental strategies. **2.NBT.5:** Fluently add and subtract within 100 using strategies based on the relationship between addition and subtraction. **2.NBT.9:** Explain why addition and subtraction strategies work, using place value and the properties of operations.	• Understand various meanings of addition and subtraction of whole numbers and the relationship between the two operations. • Understand the effects of adding and subtracting whole numbers. • Develop and use strategies for whole-number computations, with a focus on addition and subtraction. • Develop fluency with basic number combinations for addition and subtraction.
Adding Three Numbers, Parts 1 and 2	**2.OA.2:** Fluently add and subtract within 20 using mental strategies. **2.NBT.9:** Explain why addition and subtraction strategies work, using place value and the properties of operations.	• Understand various meanings of addition and subtraction of whole numbers and the relationship between the two operations. • Understand the effects of adding and subtracting whole numbers. • Develop and use strategies for whole-number computations, with a focus on addition and subtraction. • Develop fluency with basic number combinations for addition and subtraction.
Adding by Expanding Numbers	**2.NBT.5:** Fluently add and subtract within 100 using strategies based on place value, properties of operations, and/or the relationship between addition and subtraction. **2.NBT.6:** Add up to four two-digit numbers using strategies based on place value and properties of operations. **2.NBT.9:** Explain why addition and subtraction strategies work, using place value and the properties of operations. **3.NBT.2:** Fluently add and subtract within 1000 using strategies and algorithms based on place value, properties of operations, and/or the relationship between addition and subtraction.	• Understand various meanings of addition and subtraction of whole numbers and the relationship between the two operations. • Understand the effects of adding and subtracting whole numbers. • Develop and use strategies for whole-number computations, with a focus on addition and subtraction. • Develop fluency with basic number combinations for addition and subtraction. • Use a variety of methods and tools to computer, including objects, mental computation, estimation, paper and pencil, and calculators.

Making Easy Tens	**2.0A.2:** Fluently add and subtract within 20 using mental strategies. **2.NBT.5:** Fluently add and subtract within 100 using strategies based on place value, properties of operations, and/or the relationship between addition and subtraction. **2.NBT.6:** Add up to four two-digit numbers using strategies based on place value and properties of operations. **3.NBT.2:** Fluently add and subtract within 1000 using strategies and algorithms based on place value, properties of operations, and/or the relationship between addition and subtraction.	• Understand various meanings of addition and subtraction of whole numbers and the relationship between the two operations. • Understand the effects of adding and subtracting whole numbers. • Develop and use strategies for whole-number computations, with a focus on addition and subtraction. • Develop fluency with basic number combinations for addition and subtraction. • Use a variety of methods and tools to computer, including objects, mental computation, estimation, paper and pencil, and calculators.
Number Beads	**2.0A.2:** Fluently add and subtract within 20 using mental strategies.	• Understand various meanings of addition and subtraction of whole numbers and the relationship between the two operations. • Understand the effects of adding and subtracting whole numbers. • Develop and use strategies for whole-number computations, with a focus on addition and subtraction. • Develop fluency with basic number combinations for addition and subtraction. • Use a variety of methods and tools to computer, including objects, mental computation, estimation, paper and pencil, and calculators.
Repeated Addition; Multiplication Arrays; Multiplication Facts	**2.0A.4:** Use addition to find the total number of objects arranged in rectangular arrays with up to 5 rows and up to 5 columns; write an equation to express the total as a sum of equal addends. **3.0A.1:** Interpret products of whole numbers, e.g., interpret 5 x 7 as the total number of objects in 5 groups of 7 objects each.	• Understand situations that entail multiplication and division, such as equal groupings of objects and sharing equally. • Understand various meanings of multiplication and division. • Understand the effects of multiplying and dividing whole numbers.
2s, 5s, and 10s	**2.NBT.2:** Count within 1000; skip-count by 5s, 10s, and 100s. **3.0A.1:** Interpret products of whole numbers, e.g., interpret 5 x 7 as the total number of objects in 5 groups of 7 objects each. **3.NBT.3:** Multiply one-digit whole numbers by multiples of 10 in the range of 10–90, using strategies based on place value and properties of operations.	• Understand situations that entail multiplication and division, such as equal groupings of objects and sharing equally. • Understand various meanings of multiplication and division. • Understand the effects of multiplying and dividing whole numbers. • Develop fluency with basic number combinations for multiplication and division and use these combinations to mentally compute related problems, such as 30 x 50.
Division as Sharing; Division as Grouping	**3.0A.2:** Interpret whole-number quotients of whole numbers, e.g., interpret 56 ÷ 8 as the number of objects in each share when 56 objects are partitioned equally into 8 shares, or as a number of shares when 56 objects are partitioned into equal shares of 8 objects each. **3.0A.3:** Use multiplication and division within 100 to solve word problems in situations involving equal groups, arrays, and measurement quantities.	• Understand situations that entail multiplication and division, such as equal groupings of objects and sharing equally. • Understand various meanings of multiplication and division. • Understand the effects of multiplying and dividing whole numbers.
Totals and Change; Shopping	**2.MD.8:** Solve word problems involving dollar bills, quarters, dimes, nickels, and pennies, using $ and ¢ symbols appropriately.	• Use a variety of methods and tools to computer, including objects, mental computation, estimation, paper and pencil, and calculators.

ALGEBRA READINESS

Missing Numbers	**2.0A.1:** Use addition and subtraction within 100 to solve one- and two-step word problems involving situations of adding to, taking from, putting together, taking apart, and comparing, with unknowns in all positions. **2.NBT.5:** Fluently add and subtract within 100 using strategies based on place value, properties of operations, and/or the relationship between addition and subtraction.	• Understand various meanings of addition and subtraction of whole numbers and the relationship between the two operations. • Understand the effects of adding and subtracting whole numbers. • Develop and use strategies for whole-number computations, with a focus on addition and subtraction. • Develop fluency with basic number combinations for addition and subtraction. • Use a variety of methods and tools to compute, including objects, mental computation, estimation, paper and pencil, and calculators. • Illustrate general principles and properties of operations, such as commutativity, using specific numbers.
Odds & Evens	**2.0A.1:** Use addition and subtraction within 100 to solve one- and two-step word problems involving situations of adding to, taking from, putting together, taking apart, and comparing, with unknowns in all positions. **2.0A.3:** Determine whether a group of objects has an odd or even number of members.	• Develop a sense of whole numbers and represent and use them in flexible ways, including relating, composing, and decomposing numbers. • Develop fluency with basic number combinations for addition and subtraction. • Model situations that involve the addition and subtraction of whole numbers, using objects, pictures, and symbols.
Figure It Out; Money Problems	**2.0A.1:** Use addition and subtraction within 100 to solve one- and two-step word problems involving situations of adding to, taking from, putting together, taking apart, and comparing, with unknowns in all positions. **3.0A.3:** Use multiplication and division within 100 to solve word problems in situations involving equal groups, arrays, and measurement quantities. **3.0A.8:** Solve two-step word problems using the four operations. Assess the reasonableness of answers using mental computation and estimation strategies including rounding.	• Understand various meanings of addition and subtraction of whole numbers and the relationship between the two operations. • Understand the effects of adding and subtracting whole numbers. • Develop and use strategies for whole-number computations, with a focus on addition and subtraction. • Understand situations that entail multiplication and division, such as equal groupings of objects and sharing equally. • Use a variety of methods and tools to compute, including objects, mental computation, estimation, paper and pencil, and calculators. • Understand various meanings of multiplication and division. • Develop fluency in adding, subtracting, multiplying, and dividing whole numbers. • Express mathematical relationships using equations.

| Word Problems | **3.OA.3:** Use multiplication and division within 100 to solve word problems in situations involving equal groups, arrays, and measurement quantities.
3.OA.8: Solve two-step word problems using the four operations. Assess the reasonableness of answers using mental computation and estimation strategies including rounding. | • Understand various meanings of multiplication and division.
• Understand the effects of multiplying and dividing whole numbers.
• Identify and use relationships between operations, such as division as the inverse of multiplication, to solve problems.
• Develop and use strategies to estimate the results of whole-number computations and to judge the reasonableness of such results.
• Express mathematical relationships using equations.
• Model problem situations with objects and use representations such as graphs, tables, and equations to draw conclusions. |
| Sort the Aliens | n/a | • Sort, classify, and order objects by size, number, and other properties. |

MEASUREMENTS & DATA ANALYSIS

Telling Time; What Time Is It?	**2.MD.7:** Tell and write time from analog and digital clocks to the nearest five minutes, using a.m. and p.m. **3.MD.1:** Tell and write time to the nearest minute and measure time intervals in minutes. Solve word problems involving addition and subtraction of time intervals in minutes.	• Recognize the attributes of length, volume, weight, area, and time. • Compare and order objects according to this attribute.
What Do I Use to Measure?	**2.MD.1:** Measure the length of an object by selecting and using appropriate tools such as rulers, yardsticks, meter sticks, and measuring tapes. **2.MD.3:** Estimate lengths using units of inches, feet, centimeters, and meters. **3.MD.2:** Measure and estimate liquid volumes and masses of objects using standard units of grams (g), kilograms (kg), and liters (l).	• Understand such attributes as length, area, weight, volume, and size of angle and select the appropriate type of unit for measuring each attribute. • Understand the need for measuring with standard units and become familiar with standard units in the customary and metric systems. • Select and apply appropriate stand units and tools to measure length, area, volume, weight, time, temperature, and the size of angles.
Favorite Fruits and Drinks; Animals Pictogram; Colors Bar Chart	**2.MD.10:** Draw a picture graph and a bar graph (with single-unit scale) to represent a data set with up to four categories. Solve simple put-together, take-apart, and compare problems using information presented in a bar graph. **3.MD.3:** Draw a scaled picture graph and a scaled bar graph to represent a data set with several categories. Solve one- and two-step "how many more" and "how many less" problems using information presented in scaled bar graphs.	• Pose questions and gather data about themselves and their surroundings. • Represent data using concrete objects, pictures, and graphs. • Describe parts of the data and the set of data as a whole to determine what the data shows. • Design investigations to address a question and consider how data-collection methods affect the nature of the data set. • Collect data using observations, surveys, and experiments. • Represent data using tables and graphs, such as line plots, bar graphs, and line graphs.

GEOMETRY

Shape Names; Shape Sorting	**2.G.1:** Recognize and draw shapes having specified attributes, such as a given number of angles or a given number of equal faces. Identify triangles, quadrilaterals, pentagons, hexagons, and cubes.	• Recognize, name, build, draw, compare, and sort two- and three-dimensional shapes. • Describe attributes and parts of two- and three-dimensional shapes. • Identify, compare, and analyze attributes of two- and three-dimensional shapes and develop vocabulary to describe the attributes. • Classify two- and three-dimensional shapes according to their properties and develop definitions of classes of shapes such as triangles and pyramids.
Shapes and Patterns	**2.G.1:** Recognize and draw shapes having specified attributes, such as a given number of angles or a given number of equal faces. Identify triangles, quadrilaterals, pentagons, hexagons, and cubes.	• Describe attributes and parts of two- and three-dimensional shapes. • Identify, compare, and analyze attributes of two- and three-dimensional shapes and develop vocabulary to describe the attributes. • Predict and describe the results of sliding, flipping, and turning two-dimensional shapes.
Position	n/a	• Describe, name, and interpret relative positions in space and apply ideas about relative position. • Find and name locations with simple relationships such as "near to" and in coordinate systems such as maps. • Recognize geometric shapes and structures in the environment and specify their location. • Describe location and movement using common language and geometric vocabulary.
Moving Along a Route	n/a	• Describe, name, and interpret direction and distance in navigating space and apply ideas about direction and distance. • Describe location and movement using common language and geometric vocabulary.
Spot the Right Angle	n/a	• Recognize and apply slides, flips, and turns. • Recognize geometric shapes and structures in the environment and specify their location. • Develop common referents for measures to make comparisons and estimates. • Understand such attributes as the size of angle and select the appropriate type of unit for measuring each attribute. • Select and apply appropriate standard units and tools to measure the size of angles.
Reflections; Line of Symmetry	n/a	• Recognize and create shapes that have symmetry.

Counting in Tens and Ones

Learning objectives
- Read and write two-digit numbers in figures and words.
- Describe and extend number sequences.

Resources
- "Counting in Tens and Ones" Notebook file
- "Fill in the Numbers" (page 51)
- 0–100 number cards, in a bag
- 4 index cards with written instructions (*count on in ones*; *count back in ones*; *count on in tens*; *count back in tens*), in a bag

Whiteboard tools
- Pen tray
- Select tool
- Highlighter pen

Getting Started
Open page 2 of the "Counting in Tens and Ones" Notebook file. Press on the thumbnail image to open the *Number Grid Interactive Teaching Program* and highlight two numbers by clicking on them. Count in ones from the lower to the higher number and back again. Challenge more-confident learners to complete the task without looking at the grid.

Now, choose two numbers that are an exact multiple of 10 apart (for example, 24 and 84) and count in tens from the lower to the higher number and back again. Ask: *What pattern do the numbers follow on the 100-square?* Show that they go vertically down a column.

Mini-Lesson
1. Use the *Number Grid Interactive Teaching Program* to highlight patterns in the numbers when counting forward and backward in ones and tens.

2. Ask: *What patterns can you see in the numbers?* Explain that, when counting in ones, the ones digit increases or decreases by one every step, but the tens digit remains constant—except when the count passes a multiple of 10. Explain also that, when counting in tens, the ones digit remains constant, but the tens digit increases or decreases by one every step.

3. Check that students understand that when counting forward in ones or tens, you are adding 1 or 10, and when counting backward in ones or tens, you are subtracting 1 or 10.

4. Go to page 3 of the Notebook file and look at the number sequence. Ask students to tell you which number is missing from the sequence. How do they know? Highlight the numbers on the 100-square grid, if required. If desired, use voting methods to decide on the correct answer. Drag the chosen number to the sequence to check whether it is correct or not.

5. Repeat this process for pages 4 to 12. Use these sequences to assess understanding and tackle any misconceptions.

Independent Work
Divide the class into small groups and give each group a copy of "Fill in the Numbers" (p. 51). Ask students to fill in the missing numbers. Remind them to use their findings about the patterns created by counting on and back in tens and ones to help them check their answers.

Wrap-Up
Sit in a circle and pass around the two bags of cards to music (see Resources). When the music stops, the student holding the bags takes out a card from each bag and reads it to the class. Explain that the number card gives the starting number and the instruction card states how to count until the student has walked around the circle once and is back at his or her place. During this activity, take the opportunity to assess students' understanding.

Expanding Numbers

Learning objectives
- Explain what each digit in a two-digit number represents, including numbers where 0 is a placeholder.
- Expand two-digit numbers in different ways, including into multiples of 10 and 1.

Resources
- "Expanding Numbers" Notebook file
- "Arrow Number Cards" (p. 52), copied onto cardstock and cut apart
- base-ten blocks
- pencils
- paper
- individual whiteboards and pens

Whiteboard tools
- Pen tray
- Select tool

Getting Started
Open the "Expanding Numbers" Notebook file and go to page 2. Read the number words and numerals together. Order the numerals down the page from smallest to largest. Ask: *How do we know that this is the smallest/largest number?* Establish that to order the numbers you need to look at the first digit; the second digit is only looked at if two numbers have the same first digit. Finally, match the words to the numerals by dragging and dropping them into position on the screen.

Mini-Lesson
1. Show students a 10 and a 1 from the base-ten blocks. Ensure that they understand what both pieces are worth.

2. Display page 3 of the Notebook file. Explain that "expanding a number" means showing what each digit is worth. Tell students that they are going to learn how to expand numbers into tens and ones.

3. Ask a student to move ten of the orange unit squares to the middle of the screen to build a tower. Let two other students repeat the exercise. Count the three sticks of 10 to show that there are 30 ones. Elicit that 30 ones make 3 tens. Ask: *How do we make the number 36?* Reveal the answer on page 4 after everyone has shared his or her ideas.

4. Give out base-ten blocks and instruct students to make the number 52. Ask a student to choose the correct answer on page 5. Press on the image that they think is right to produce a groan or cheer depending on whether or not the answer is correct. Repeat this for number 37 on page 6.

5. Give out Arrow Number Cards (p. 52) and instruct students to make the numbers displayed on page 7. Invite a student to move the arrow cards on the board.

6. As an assessment, allow students to investigate the numbers on page 8 using the base-ten blocks and the arrow cards. Allow students to demonstrate their work on page 8. Press the button to go to the answers on page 9.

Independent Work
Divide the class into small groups. Give each group a set of two-digit numbers to expand into tens and ones. Suggest ways that they could record their work, either as a sum or pictorially (for example: 35 = 3 tens + 5 ones).

Let less-confident learners work practically with support, making two-digit numbers with base-ten blocks and arrow cards. Challenge more-confident learners to partition three-digit numbers into hundreds, tens, and ones.

Wrap-Up
Look at the numbers on page 10 of the Notebook file. Ask students to expand one of the numbers on their individual whiteboards. Address any errors made. Look at the number 30. Ask: *How many tens and ones is this number made from?* Explain the importance of the zero—it changes the value of the 3 from 3 ones to 3 tens.

Ordering Numbers

Learning objective
- Read, write, and order whole numbers to at least 1,000 and position them on a number line.

Resources
- "Ordering Numbers" Notebook file
- number lines
- individual whiteboards and pens
- sets of ten numbers
- paper and glue

Whiteboard tools
- Pen tray
- Select tool
- On-screen Keyboard
- Text tool

Getting Started

Load the *Number Line Interactive Teaching Program* on page 2 of the "Ordering Numbers" Notebook file. Set the upper number of the number line to 100 (click on the right arrow on the "max" icon) and ask students to identify the position of numbers along the number line. Later, extend this to 500. Ask questions such as: *If this is 200 and this is 250, by how much are the little tick marks increasing?* Hide the numbers on the scale (click on the icon with 00) and ask students to identify different marks along the line.

Mini-Lesson

1. Read the numbers on page 3 of the Notebook file out loud. Ask students if they notice anything about the numbers. Lead them to understand that there are ten consecutive numbers but they are not in the correct order.

2. Ask one student to come to the SMART Board to select the highest number in the set and drag it to the corresponding position on the line.

3. Repeat this with another student, selecting the lowest number, middle numbers, and so on.

4. Go to page 4. On this page are ten more consecutive numbers that bridge a hundreds number (300). However, they are not in order. With students, position the numbers in order on the number line. If students struggle with placing these numbers (from their nonsequential positions), support them in identifying the smallest number and help them count up from that number.

5. Page 5 features ten numbers between 150 and 210. Ask students to order these numbers along an empty number line.

6. On individual whiteboards or paper, ask students to suggest a number that could be added to this set of numbers. Challenge more-confident learners to record all the numbers in order, to make this a complete sequential set.

Independent Work

Give each student a number line and a set of ten number cards (consecutively bridging a tens number for less-confident learners, and nonconsecutively bridging a hundreds number for more-confident learners). Ask them to position or glue the numbers onto the blank number line. Alternatively, let them record the completed number line in their notebooks. Students should then fill in the missing numbers to complete the nonconsecutive lines and read the numbers to a partner.

Wrap-Up

Go to page 6 of the Notebook file. Use the Random Number Generator to generate ten random three-digit numbers. (Write the numbers in the space provided.) Ask students to order them from largest to smallest and record them on their individual whiteboards. Encourage them to show their whiteboards, or invite a student to order the numbers on the SMART Board.

Count around the class, starting at 470 then over and back from 500. Continue the exercise starting at 854 and bridging 900. Discuss any misconceptions if there are any incorrect answers.

Hundreds, Tens, and Ones

Learning objectives
- Read, write, and order whole numbers to at least 1,000.
- Expand three-digit numbers into multiples of 100, 10, and 1 in different ways.

Resources
- "Hundreds, Tens, and Ones" Notebook file
- "Hundreds, Tens, and Ones" (p. 53)
- writing materials

Whiteboard tools
- Pen tray
- Select tool
- Delete button

Getting Started
Display the number grid on page 2 of the "Hundreds, Tens, and Ones" Notebook file. One row and one column have been hidden. Ask students to figure out the missing numbers. When they suggest a missing number, press on the relevant rectangle and delete the colored block to reveal the number. Ask students how they figured out the missing number. Did they count on or back in ones or in tens? Extend the activity by pressing on the Starter extension button, which reveals a hidden 5 x 5 square of numbers, bridging tens numbers and 100. Encourage students to count on in fives.

Mini-Lesson
1. Look at the number grid on page 2 or 3 of the Notebook file. Ask students to generate facts they know about the grid. For example, as the numbers go down a column, the numbers increase by ten, so the tens number changes, but the ones (or units) number stays the same.

2. Display the hundreds, tens, and ones table on page 4. Write a tens number and a ones number in the appropriate columns and ask a volunteer to write a two-digit whole number (the integer) on the SMART Board and read it out.

3. Call out some two- and three-digit numbers and ask students to write down the hundreds, tens, and ones numbers. Invite volunteers to write their answers in the table on the SMART Board.

Independent Work
Using a copy of "Hundreds, Tens, and Ones" (p. 53), ask students to lightly color in a hundreds, a tens, and a ones (or units) number. Have them swap sheets with a partner, who must write out the hundreds, tens, and ones numbers as well as the completed three-digit number in their notebook. Repeat a few times, ensuring that students understand the place value of each of the digits.

For less-confident learners, limit this activity to two-digit numbers. Show them how to cut out the number cards and place them over each other to find the completed number.

Wrap-Up
Discuss any numbers that students found difficult to represent using place value cards (such as 406). Go to page 5 of the Notebook file and open the *Place Value Interactive Teaching Program*. Drag the bottom-right corner to resize the pop-up window. Press the farthest left of the three arrows until 400 appears in the window, then press 400. A number card for 400 will appear on screen. Repeat this process with 6 in the third window. Discuss what needs to be pressed to reveal the tens number (the middle window). Once the number is displayed on-screen, drag each part of the number apart to show 400 and 0 and 6. The arrow at the bottom of the place value numbers shows the number represented by red beads.

Base-10 Numbers

Learning objectives
- Read, write, and order whole numbers to at least 1,000.
- Expand three-digit numbers into multiples of 100, 10, and 1 in different ways.

Resources
- "Base-10 Numbers" Notebook file
- base-ten cubes (ones, tens, hundreds, and thousands cubes)
- place-value board
- individual whiteboards and pens

Whiteboard tools
- Pen tray
- Select tool
- Highlighter pen
- Undo button
- Delete button

Getting Started
Display page 2 of the "Base-10 Numbers" Notebook file. Ask the class to count, in turn, the hundreds numbers, the tens, and the ones (or units). Highlight a tens number and a ones number. Invite a student to write the two-digit number that it produces on-screen and read it aloud. Press the Undo button until the page has been reset and repeat for a three-digit number. Go to page 3 and use the Fill Color tool to fill one of the yellow boxes to reveal a number. Ask students to make the given number using the hundreds, tens, and ones on the page.

Mini-Lesson
1. Go to page 4 of the Notebook file. Point out the numeral 1 and ask students how it could be shown with base-ten blocks. Reveal the base-ten block by deleting the red panel.

2. Ask students what the blocks under the 10 will look like. Again, delete the rectangle to reveal the shape beneath it.

3. Repeat with 100 and 1,000. Point out that 100 is shown by ten blocks across and ten blocks down (10 x 10 = 100), and 1,000 by ten layers of 100 squares (10 x 100 = 1000).

4. Write a three-digit number in the box on page 5. Ask students to read the number aloud. Prompt them to consider place value, with questions such as: *How many hundreds are in the number? Which digit represents the tens number?*

5. Ask students to drag the correct number of base-ten cubes to the center of the page to represent this number. Ask the rest of the class to check whether or not they are correct.

6. Reset the page by using the Undo button and repeat with other numbers such as 999 or 600.

Independent Work
Working in pairs, have partners take turns writing a two- or three-digit number on their whiteboard, while the other represents it using base-ten cubes. Reverse the activity: one student selects a number of hundreds, tens, and ones blocks, and the other has to write down the number represented. This activity can be extended to include base-ten cubes to 1,000 or simplified to numbers less than 100.

Wrap-Up
Ask students to demonstrate the numbers they have made, especially if anyone made numbers over 1,000. Using a student's example of a three-digit number, ask the class what they would need to do to add 10. For example, 188 would be represented by one 100-square, eight 10-sticks, and eight 1-cubes. Add a 10-stick to the eight 10-sticks and discuss why the hundreds and tens numbers remain the same. Challenge the class to think about the effects of adding another 10. *What would change? Could the number be represented differently using the base-ten blocks?* This can be modeled on page 5 of the Notebook file. Repeat with subtracting 1, 10, or 100.

Number Facts

Learning objective
- Derive and recall all addition and subtraction facts for each number to at least 10.

Resources
- "Number Facts" Notebook file
- "Four in a Row" (p. 54)
- "Fact Cards" (p. 55), copied onto cardstock and cut apart
- 2 index cards with plus and minus symbols
- counters in two different colors
- individual whiteboards and pens
- whistle

Whiteboard tools
- Pen tray
- Select tool
- On-screen Keyboard

(Microsoft Excel is required to view the embedded spreadsheet in the Notebook file. Prior to opening the Excel file, ensure that your Excel security level is set to Medium [Tools menu > Macro submenu > Security command]. You will be prompted to enable or disable macros when you open the "Missing Numbers" Excel file; choose "Enable macros" for this file to work properly.)

Getting Started

Open the "Number Facts" Notebook file. Go to page 3 and press the icon to launch the Excel file. Choose the tab labeled "addition 4" at the bottom of the spreadsheet. Set the number after the equals sign to any number between 0 and 10 using the arrows beneath the number or by typing it in. (Use the On-screen Keyboard, accessed through the Pen tray or the SMART Board tools menu, to input numbers in the spreadsheet cells.) On their individual whiteboards, ask students to write down two numbers that would make the number sentence correct. Type some answers on the SMART Board to check them. Next, choose the tab at the bottom labeled "subtraction 4" and repeat the activity, this time finding two numbers to subtract to make the number sentence correct.

Mini-Lesson

1. Return to the Notebook file and go to page 4. Press the thumbnail image to open the *Number Spinners Interactive Teaching Program*. Click on the up arrow of the icon with the white triangle in the center to change the shape to a hexagon. Then click on the up arrow of the icon next to it to change the number to 2. Click on the first icon again to display two six-sided spinners.

2. Invite one student to press the center of each spinner, then ask another student to read the two numbers spun.

3. Show students a plus or minus symbol on a card to let them know whether to add or subtract the two numbers. Encourage them to show the answers using their fingers. Give them only a few seconds before you ask for an answer.

Independent Work

Provide each pair of children with an enlarged copy of "Four in a Row" (p. 54), together with a prepared spinner (from the reproducible) and several counters in two different colors. Explain that the object of the game is to be the first player to get four counters in a row on the board, horizontally, vertically, or diagonally. Show examples of winning lines so that there is no confusion. Explain the rules as given on the sheet. Let students check their opponent's calculations and encourage them to contest dubious answers.

Allow less-confident learners to use cubes or a number line to help check their addition and subtraction. As an extension, provide more-confident learners with an adapted game that uses the results of two spinners added together to make the target number and includes numbers up to 20 on the game board.

Wrap-Up

Hold up cards from "Fact Cards" (p. 55). Give students a few seconds to figure out the answer, then blow a whistle to signal that students need to get into groups of that amount. This activity needs a large space for students to move around safely. As an added challenge, ask any group that did not manage to find enough children how many more children they need in their group.

Inverse Operations

Learning objective
- Understand that subtraction is the inverse of addition and vice versa, and use this to derive and record related addition and subtraction number sentences.

Resources
- "Inverse Operations" Notebook file
- "Number Triplets" (p. 56)
- individual whiteboards and pens
- large index cards

Whiteboard tools
- Pen tray
- Select tool
(Microsoft PowerPoint is required to view the embedded slideshow in the Notebook file.)

Before You Start
Prepare "inverse partner" game cards for the Wrap-Up activity: Using large index cards, write an addition problem on each card and a corresponding subtraction problem on another card (for example, 12 + 16 = 28 and 28 – 16 = 12).

Getting Started
Open page 2 of the "Inverse Operations" Notebook file. Talk about different strategies for solving addition and subtraction problems. Provide each student with an individual whiteboard. Call out five simple addition and subtraction problems. Allow sufficient time after calling out each question for students to figure out and record the answers on their boards. Share the answers and strategies used to find them.

Mini-Lesson
1. Show page 3 of the Notebook file. Pull the tabs and read the text. Explain that the term *inverse* means "reverse" or "opposite."

2. Press the link at the top of the page to open the PowerPoint presentation to demonstrate that addition is indeed the inverse of subtraction and vice versa. Investigate further on a number line.

3. Return to the Notebook file and show page 4. Give students one minute to write down as many inverses of the number sentences as they can.

4. Once students have a clear understanding of inverse operations, move on to page 5 to introduce the idea that this understanding can be used to solve problems.

5. Using the ladybug on page 6 with a number of spots on each wing, show students how the spots give two addition equations. Write the equations on the page. Encourage students to use their knowledge of inverse operations to work out the corresponding subtraction equations. Once they have done this, pull out the tab to reveal the answers.

6. Provide students with an opportunity to repeat this task independently on page 7.

7. Go to page 8. Show students how a set of three numbers can make two addition and two subtraction equations. Pull out the tab to reveal the answers.

8. Provide students with an opportunity to repeat this procedure independently on page 9.

Independent Work
Divide the class into small groups. Provide each group with a set of "Number Triplets" (p. 56). Change the numbers on the cards, if necessary, so that they are within a range that students are comfortable working with. Ask students to create two addition and two subtraction equations using the three numbers on each card. Remind students that if they find two addition equations, they can use their knowledge of inverse operations to find the subtraction equations.

Wrap-Up
Talk about any problems that students encountered during their work and solve them together, using page 10 of the Notebook file for notes. Give each student a card with either an addition or subtraction sentence on it (see Before You Start). Take students into a large space and ask them to find their inverse partners.

Adding Three Numbers, Part 1

Learning objectives

- Derive and recall all addition facts for each number to at least 10, all pairs with totals to 20.
- Use knowledge of number facts.

Resources

- "Adding Three Numbers, Part 1" Notebook file
- 0–20 number cards for each group
- individual whiteboards and pens

Whiteboard tools

- Pen tray
- Select tool
- Delete button

Getting Started

Open the *Number Spinners Interactive Teaching Program* from page 2 of the "Adding Three Numbers, Part 1" Notebook file. Click on the up arrow of the icon with the white triangle in the center to change the shape to a hexagon. Then click on the up arrow of the icon next to it to change the number to 2. Click on the first icon again to display two six-sided spinners.

Invite a volunteer to spin both spinners and ask students to add the two numbers together as quickly as they can. Talk about the strategies they can use to work out the answers quickly if they do not know the number fact by heart (for example, solve 5 + 6 by using their knowledge that double 5 is 10, then adding 1 more).

Mini-Lesson

1. Use page 3 of the Notebook file to introduce the strategy of adding three numbers by putting the largest first. Move the numbers into the correct order. Emphasize that putting the largest number first is a useful strategy because it means there is less to add on and therefore less room for errors to be made in calculating the answer.

2. Ask students to write the number sentence on individual whiteboards and then work out the answer. Invite a student to come to the SMART Board to write the answer on the screen in the space provided. To check the student's answer, use the Eraser from the Pen tray to rub over the white box to show the correct answer.

3. Repeat this activity on page 4.

4. Use pages 5 and 6 to assess students' understanding. On page 5, ask students to rewrite the addition number sentences with the largest number first and then solve them. Invite one of students to come to the SMART Board to move the numbers into the correct order.

5. Go to page 6 to confirm the order of the numbers. Invite students to come to the board to complete the addition sentences on-screen. Then use the Delete button to remove the red boxes to show the correct answers.

Independent Work

Give each group a set of 0–20 number cards. Ask students to pick three numbers and add them together. (Give less-confident learners a set of 0–10 cards and more-confident learners a set of 0–30 cards.) Encourage students to order the three chosen number cards from largest to smallest, write the addition sentence, and solve the problem.

Wrap-Up

Display page 7 of the Notebook file and ask a student to read out the number sentence. Instruct students to explain to a partner how they would work out the answer. Share some of these ideas. Ask a student to rearrange the equation to show the largest number first. Invite another student to share their strategy for working out the sum and let them write in the answer.

Adding Three Numbers, Part 2

Learning objective
- Derive and recall all addition facts for each number to at least 10.

Resources
- "Adding Three Numbers, Part 2" Notebook file
- "Ladybug Flip Flap" (p. 57)
- "Adding on to Ten" (p. 58)
- individual whiteboards and pens

Whiteboard tools
- Pen tray
- Highlighter pen
- Select tool
- Delete button

Getting Started

Give each student a copy of the "Ladybug Flip Flap" (p. 57). Say a number between 0 and 10 and ask students to show that amount of ladybugs using their flip flap. When students are comfortable with this, ask them to show the number that needs to be added to the number you say in order to make 10. For example, if you say 7, students should show 3 ladybugs.

Mini-Lesson

1. Go to page 2 of the "Adding Three Numbers, Part 2" Notebook file. Show students the number sentence. Ask: *What could you do to find the answer?*

2. Use the Delete button to reveal the clue. Remind students of the Getting Started activity, where they were finding numbers that equal 10.

3. Point out that adding 6 and 4 gives 10, and explain that it is easier to add a number on to 10. Highlight the 6 and the 4.

4. Invite a student to come to the SMART Board to move the third number down to add to the 10 and complete the equation. Let them write in the sum. Once they have done this, delete the red box to reveal the correct answer.

5. Practice the new strategy together on page 3. Ask students to rewrite the equation on their individual whiteboards. Delete the red box to reveal the new equation. Invite one of the students to complete the equation.

6. Use page 4 for assessment. Give students one minute to solve two problems from those given, using the new strategy, and record their answers on their whiteboards.

7. Invite students to come to the SMART Board and highlight the numbers they added together first to get 10 or 20. Invite others to write in the answers. Reveal the answers by using the Eraser from the Pen tray to rub over the red boxes beneath the number sentences.

Independent Work

Give each student a copy of "Adding on to 10" (p. 58). Ask students to identify, and mark on the sheet, the problems they can solve using the strategy of finding a pair totaling 10. Tell students to put a circle around the two numbers that total 10 in each of these sums and then work out the answers.

Wrap-Up

Talk with students about which equations they solved using the strategy of finding a pair totaling 10 and which ones needed a different strategy. Ask: *How could we solve the other sums?* Make a note of students' responses on page 5 of the Notebook file. Demonstrate that it is possible to look for any multiple of 10 when adding three numbers, so the strategy can also be useful when adding three larger numbers.

Adding by Expanding Numbers

Learning objective
- Expand two-digit numbers in different ways, including into multiples of ten and one.

Resources
- "Adding by Expanding Numbers" Notebook file
- "Arrow Number Cards" (p. 52)
- 0–100 number cards
- individual whiteboards and pens
- base-ten blocks
- large index cards
- six numbers between 0 and 100 written on large paper (see Wrap-Up)

Whiteboard tools
- Pen tray
- Select tool
- Delete button

Before You Start
Using large index cards, prepare some addition equations for each group of students. Make sure the equations can be solved using the new strategy being taught in this mini-lesson.

Getting Started
Go to page 2 of the "Adding by Expanding Numbers" Notebook file. Give each student a set of Arrow Number Cards (p. 52) and challenge students to use them to make specific two-digit numbers. Ask questions such as: *How many tens are there in 35? How many ones are there in 54? Can you think of a number that has three tens?* Make notes on the Notebook page, if necessary.

Mini-Lesson
1. Explain to students that expanding numbers is a good strategy to use when adding two-digit numbers together because they can be added in parts. Use page 3 of the Notebook file to demonstrate and talk through the expanding and recombining strategy. Drag the arrow cards into place, firstly to $10 + 3 + 10 + 6$, and then to $10 + 10 + 3 + 6$. Write the sum of the tens and ones numbers in the orange and green arrows, respectively. With students, work out and write the answer.

2. Reinforce the strategy with the equations on pages 4 and 5. Give students individual whiteboards so that they can attempt to figure out the answers themselves before completing the process on-screen.

3. Encourage students to ask questions and ensure that they are following what is happening by asking them to explain the strategy. If students are finding the strategy difficult, use base-ten blocks to show the two numbers being partitioned into tens and ones and then recombined as a group of tens and a group of ones.

4. Invite a student to come to the SMART Board and drag the arrow cards on the screen, firstly to expand them and then to recombine as a group of tens and a group of ones. Invite another student to write in the answer.

5. Use pages 6 and 7 to assess students' understanding. Take this opportunity to address any errors and misconceptions. Time students to add an extra challenge to the activity.

Independent Work
Give students prepared cards with addition equations (see Before You Start). Allow them to use their Arrow Number Cards to help them. Talk with students about how they are figuring out the answers and regularly refer back to the whole-class work.

Supply less-confident learners with base-ten blocks so that they can practically partition and recombine the numbers. Challenge more-confident learners by giving them addition equations that cross the tens boundary, such as $36 + 48$.

Wrap-Up
In the hallway, stick six different numbers between 0 and 100 on the wall so that all of the students can see them. Sit students in the middle and call out an addition equation that gives one of the answers displayed on the wall. Give students adequate thinking time and then ask them to go to the number they think is the answer. Provide individual whiteboards for students to use for figuring out if they need to.

Making Easy Tens

Learning objectives

- Add or subtract mentally a single-digit number or a multiple of 10 to or from any two-digit number.
- Use practical and informal written methods to add and subtract two-digit numbers.

Resources

- "Making Easy Tens" Notebook file
- "Making Easy 10s" (p. 59)
- individual whiteboards and pens
- cubes or other counters

Whiteboard tools

- Pen tray
- Select tool *(Microsoft PowerPoint is required to view the embedded slideshow in the Notebook file.)*

Getting Started

Refresh and build on students' knowledge of simple addition. Record addition facts to 10 on page 2 of the "Making Easy Tens" Notebook file, and use page 3 to review addition facts for numbers up to 10. Ask students to list their strategies for each task on their individual whiteboards. Then invite volunteers to come to the SMART Board and write their answers on the Notebook page.

Mini-Lesson

1. Ensure that students know what a multiple of 10 is.

2. Launch the slideshow on page 4 of the Notebook file to explain and demonstrate the method of addition by "making easy tens" (see slides 1 to 4).

3. Demonstrate clearly that 8 + 6 is the same amount as 10 + 4. Give one student eight cubes and another student six cubes. Ask the student with six cubes to give two of them to the student with eight cubes and then point out that this now shows 10 + 4 = 14. Ask: *Has the number of cubes changed?*

4. Use the PowerPoint slideshow (slides 5 to 10) to solve three addition problems using the method of making easy tens. Encourage students to work in pairs on their individual whiteboards to work out each step.

5. On page 4 of the Notebook file, demonstrate how students should record each step of the newly learned strategy. Encourage them to practice this on their individual whiteboards. For example: 8 + 6 = 8 + 2 + 4 = 10 + 4 = 14.

6. Encourage students to use their preferred method (such as counting on) to check the answer to increase their confidence in the reliability of the new method.

7. Finally, use page 5 to assess understanding. Let each student choose a problem to solve independently.

Independent Work

Give each student a copy of "Making Easy 10s" (p. 59). (You can differentiate by giving less-confident learners only the problems on the left side of the page.) Have students choose at least five of the problems to solve using the method of making easy tens and then solve them, recording their answers as demonstrated. Provide less-confident learners with a number line and additional teacher support. Encourage students to explain to a partner how they solved each of the questions. Allow students to check their work using their preferred method of addition.

Wrap-Up

Ask students to share any successes and difficulties they have experienced and work through an example as a class. Use page 6 of the Notebook file or look again at the last two slides of the slideshow (slides 9 and 10: *What is 16 + 7?*) to help students assimilate their new knowledge. Drag and drop the blocks and change the numbers on the arrow cards. In a subsequent lesson, when students are comfortable with addition by making easy tens, use pages 7 to 8 to introduce the method of subtraction using the same strategy.

Number Beads

Learning objective

- Derive and recall all addition and subtraction facts for each number to 20.

Resources

- "Number Beads" Notebook file
- set of bead strings per pair of students (20 beads or dry macaroni on a string)
- 0–20 number cards
- individual whiteboards and pens

Whiteboard tools

- Pen tray
- Select tool
- Undo button

Getting Started

Open the *Number Facts Interactive Teaching Program* on page 2 of the "Number Beads" Notebook file. Press on the *plus* (+) symbol to activate a minus calculation and select the bin option. Switch off the number sentence function (click on the button with ? + ? =).

Start by showing the ten purple beads. Ask students what subtraction fact is shown if nine beads are dropped into the bin. (The number sentence should be hidden.) Question how this subtraction fact could be recorded. Ask students to write this on their individual whiteboards before revealing it on-screen (click on ? + ? =). Repeat with a subtraction fact from 10. The purple spots will change to yellow as they are added to the bin; encourage students to watch the changes to the number sentence.

Mini-Lesson

1. Go to page 3 of the Notebook file. On the page are two sets of 20-bead strings. Each set of ten is represented by a different color to aid in adding and subtracting numbers larger than 10.

2. Discuss what the two colors represent and establish that there are ten beads of each color. Drag across ten beads of one color (select all ten beads to move them as a group) and one bead of the other color. Ask students to use their understanding of place value and work out what is being represented. Record this as an addition sentence (10 + 1 = 11). Repeat with other addition facts up to 20.

3. Start at 20 beads and pull 18 back toward the left. Write it as a number sentence (20 − 18 = 2).

4. Ask students to discuss similarities and differences with the previous addition sentences. By taking away beads, you are showing a subtraction fact.

5. Use the Undo button to reset the page and repeat this process with other subtraction facts from 20.

Independent Work

Provide pairs of students with a set of number cards and a string of beads. Working in pairs, have one student turn over a number card and make this number on a string of beads. Have the partner record this number and figure out the addend to get to 20. For example, with a number card for 12, one student drags across 12 beads, and the other works out that 12 + 8 = 20. Then have them swap roles. This activity can be extended or simplified using higher or lower addition facts and sets of number cards. After recording ten addition facts, have the pairs repeat the activity with subtraction facts. For example, if 11 is on the cards, 11 beads are pulled away from 20. The subtraction sentence will be 20 − 11 = 9.

Wrap-Up

Ask some children to demonstrate different addition or subtraction facts. This can be done using the bead string on the SMART Board or their own bead string on the table. Write their examples of number sentences on page 4 of the Notebook file.

Repeated Addition

Learning objective
- Represent repeated addition as multiplication.

Resources
- "Repeated Addition" Notebook file
- "Multiply by Adding" (p. 60), copied onto cardstock and cut apart
- counters
- individual whiteboards and pens

Whiteboard tools
- Pen tray
- Select tool
- On-screen Keyboard
- Area Capture tool
- Undo button
(Microsoft PowerPoint is required to view the embedded slideshow in the Notebook file.)

Getting Started

Go to page 2 of the "Repeated Addition" Notebook file. Open the *Number Grid Interactive Teaching Program* and ask students to highlight all the multiples of 2 (simply click the numbers). Use the grid to count in twos from 0 to 100.

Next, ask students to highlight all the multiples of 5. Use the grid to count in fives from 0 to 100. Finally, ask students to highlight all the multiples of 10. Use the grid to count in tens from 0 to 100.

Mini-Lesson

1. Tell students that they are going to learn how to do a new operation called *multiplication*. Explain that when you multiply, you are adding a number to itself a certain number of times.

2. Open the slideshow on page 3 of the Notebook file. Use slides 1 to 4 to introduce the multiplication symbol, the terminology used to read a multiplication equation, and the term *repeated addition*.

3. Show students how to do repeated addition for a multiplication equation using slides 5 and 6.

4. Supply counters for students. Display slide 7 and ask them to work out the answers to the multiplication problems by making groups. Translate the groups of counters into number sentences and ask some children to type the number sentences into the boxes. (Use the On-screen Keyboard, accessed through the Pen tray or the SMART Board tools menu, to type in numbers.)

5. Show students slides 8 and 9 so that they can check their answers.

6. Use the Area Capture tool to take screenshots of slideshow pages, if necessary.

Independent Work

Give each group a set of the "Multiply by Adding" cards (p. 60). Tell students to choose a card, read the multiplication fact, and then write it as a repeated addition. Allow students to use counters and number lines for support during the lesson.

Work with less-confident learners to help them make groups of counters. For example, for 2 x 6, make six groups of 2. Challenge more-confident learners by including some 3- and 4-times table problems.

Wrap-Up

Return to the Notebook file and display page 4. Drag and drop a number of one type of fruit into the white box on the page. Give students individual whiteboards. Ask them to use their boards to figure out how much it would cost to buy the items shown on the Notebook page. Once they have done this, use the Undo button to reset the page. Display another set of fruit and ask students to calculate the cost of this new set. Provide opportunities for students to explain how they worked out their answers. Ensure they understand they are multiplying the amounts using repeated addition to work out the answers.

Multiplication Arrays

Learning objective
- Represent repeated arrays as multiplication.

Resources
- "Multiplication Arrays" Notebook file
- several pennies, nickels, and dimes
- counters
- paper
- pencils
- index cards

Whiteboard tools
- Pen tray
- Select tool

(Microsoft PowerPoint is required to view the embedded slideshow in the Notebook file.)

Before You Start
Write a set of multiplication problems (facts without products) on index cards for each group of students. Use facts from 2-, 5-, and 10-times tables.

Getting Started
Open the "Multiplication Arrays" Notebook file and go to page 2. Ask students to work out how much money is on pages 2, 3, and 4. Encourage them to count in ones, fives, or tens accordingly. Put some pennies, nickels, and dimes on each table and ask students to make given amounts using a particular coin or coins. Ask how many of each coin students needed to make the given amount.

Mini-Lesson
1. Go to page 5 of the Notebook file and ask: *What do we already know about multiplication?*

2. Open the PowerPoint slideshow. Introduce students to the idea of an *array* using slides 1 to 3. Explain that an array is a set of objects arranged into rows and columns so that they make a rectangle formation. Remind students that columns are vertical and rows are horizontal.

3. Support students in making arrays with counters to show given multiplication equations. Make some arrays with counters and ask students what number sentences the arrays are describing.

4. Display slides 4 to 15 for an opportunity to assess students' understanding. Using slide 4, ask students to choose which array the equation is describing. Press on the array to check the answer. There are three assessment questions altogether.

5. Relate the work on arrays to the work done previously on multiplication using repeated addition. Show that each row/column is identical—so by adding the total number of objects in one row/column to itself a certain number of times, a repeated addition is taking place.

Independent Work
Give each group a set of prepared cards (see Before You Start) and a set of counters. Tell students to choose a card, read it, and then make the array it describes, using the counters provided. Once students have made the array with counters, tell them to draw the array and work out the answer to the equation.

Work with less-confident learners to help them make the arrays for 2-times table problems to begin with. Challenge more-confident learners by including some 3- and 4-times table problems.

Wrap-Up
Supply a set of counters for each group. Ask one member of each group to choose a card from the set they used during Independent Work and show it to the rest of the group. Give students ten seconds to think and then challenge them to be the first in their group to use the counters to make the array that the card is describing.

Multiplication Facts

Learning objective
• Derive and recall multiplication facts for the 2- and 10-times tables.

Resources
• "Multiplication Facts" Notebook file
• "Ladybug Flip Flap" (p. 57)
• "Multiplication Bingo" (pp. 61–62)
• individual whiteboards and pens
• counters
• calculators

Whiteboard tools
• Pen tray
• Select tool
(Microsoft PowerPoint is required to view the embedded slideshow in the Notebook file.)

Before You Start
Use copies of the "Multiplication Bingo" (p. 62) to prepare a bingo card for each student, filling in the spaces with multiples of 2 and 10.

Getting Started
Open the "Multiplication Facts" Notebook file and display page 2. Show students a Ladybug Flip Flap (see p. 57 for instructions on how to make one) with some ladybugs hidden. Ask: *How many legs can you see?* Point out that each ladybug has six legs and show how students can count the legs in twos. Give each student a flip flap. Invite students to show a given number of ladybugs. Ask: *How many legs can you see?* Repeat, this time asking students for the number of spots they can see.

Mini-Lesson
1. Go to page 3 of the Notebook file and open the PowerPoint slideshow. Press on the star to practice the 2-times table.
2. Say the 2-times table as a class, using the terminology: *one two is two*; *two twos are four*; and so on. Use the slideshow to support this activity.
3. Repeat for the 10-times table, also using the slideshow.
4. Press Escape to exit the slideshow and return to the Notebook file. Show students page 4 and complete the table together. Filling in the boxes out of order makes this more challenging.
5. On individual whiteboards, ask students to write down the answers to each of the questions on page 5. Afterwards, invite volunteers to come to the SMART Board and use the Eraser from the Pen tray to reveal the answers.

Independent Work
Divide the class into small groups. Assign a caller for each group and give them a set of "Multiplication Bingo Question Cards" (p. 61). Give the rest of the group a prepared bingo card and counters for each student. Ask the caller to choose one question card at a time, read it clearly, and give the group time to figure out the answer. Tell the group to find the product and cover up the number on their bingo card with a counter, if it is present. Give the caller a calculator so that he or she can check the answers to each problem. Any wrongly covered answers can then be uncovered. Explain that the winner is the first person to get a line horizontally, vertically, or diagonally. Change the caller after each game.

Give less-confident learners 2-times table problems only; more-confident learners may also be given 5-times table problems.

Wrap-Up
Display page 6 of the Notebook file and ask: *How many spots can you see?* Count the spots in twos with students. Write down the corresponding multiplication fact (for example, five dice: 2 spots x 5 = 10 spots). Using page 7, ask students to state the multiplication fact and the product. Repeat this with the dimes on page 8.

2s, 5s, and 10s

Learning objective

- Derive and recall multiplication facts for the 2-, 5-, and 10-times tables.

Resources

- "2s, 5s, and 10s" Notebook file
- "Multiples of 2, 5, and 10" (p. 63)
- pens and large sheets of paper

Whiteboard tools

- Pen tray
- Select tool
- Pen tool
- Highlighter pen
- Delete button
- On-screen Keyboard
- Undo button

Getting Started

Open the "2s, 5s, and 10s" Notebook file and go to page 2. Count up and back to 100 in multiples of 10, then in multiples of 5. Count up and back in twos starting from any two-digit number. Delete the square covering the interactive 100-square. Ask students to repeat the counting, and change the multiples of 2 in green as they do so. (Click on the Pen tool to select different colors for values on the interactive 100-square.) Repeat with red for multiples of 5 and blue for multiples of 10. Ask students to discuss why some green squares change to red and then to blue. Talk about the created pattern and how that pattern would look on a 200-square grid.

Mini-Lesson

1. With the class, establish a definition for *multiple* on page 3 of the Notebook file. (For example, the multiple of a number is the product of that number times another number.)

2. Ask students to discuss with a partner how they recognize whether a number is a multiple of 2, 5, or 10. Write these ideas on the SMART Board.

3. On page 4, there are various two- and three-digit multiples of 2, 5, and 10. Point to a multiple of 2 and ask questions, such as: *How can we tell __ is a multiple of 2?*

4. Highlight a number ending in 0. Ask questions such as: *Is this a multiple of 2? How do you know? Is it a multiple of another times table? How do you know?*

5. Go to page 5, which shows some numbers around a sorting circle. Invite students to drag and drop a multiple of 2 into the circle.

6. Press the Undo button until the numbers return to their unsorted position. Clone the sorting circle and position it to overlap with the existing circle to form a Venn diagram.

7. Sort the numbers according to multiples of 2 and 5 and discuss where to place those numbers ending in 0 (multiples of both 2 and 5).

Independent Work

Working in small groups, have students sort a set of two- and three-digit numbers using "Multiples of 2, 5, and 10" (p. 63). Sort the given numbers into a Venn diagram with three rings and label the rings. There may be confusion over those numbers that are not a multiple of 2, 5, or 10. Encourage students to discuss whether they are multiples of other times tables. Place these numbers outside the rings. Encourage students to state that they know that *y is a multiple of x because...* .

Wrap-Up

Load the *Number Dial Interactive Teaching Program* on page 6 of the Notebook file; the number 2 should be the default number in the center. Ask students to complete the dial with the corresponding multiplication fact. Press the empty boxes to reveal the answers. Hide both inner and outer numbers by pressing on them. Ask questions such as: *If the answer is 18, what is the question?* If there is time, repeat with either the 5- or 10-times table. (Click on the icon with the number in the center and press the up arrow until you reach the desired number.) Discuss any misconceptions.

Division as Sharing

Learning objective
- Represent sharing as division.

Resources
- "Division as Sharing" Notebook file
- "Sharing" (p. 64)
- individual whiteboards and pens
- counters

Whiteboard tools
- Pen tray
- Select tool
- Delete button

Getting Started

On page 2 of the "Division as Sharing" Notebook file, open the *Number Grid Interactive Teaching Program*, and click on all the multiples of 5 to highlight them. Ask students to count in fives from 0 to 100. Tell them that these numbers are all multiples of 5 because they can all be shared into five equal groups with none left over. Show a range of numbers from 0 to 100 and ask them to say whether or not each number is a multiple of 5.

Mini-Lesson

1. Explain *division* as sharing a number into equal parts. Take 20 counters and share them equally among yourself and three children. Say: *I have divided the counters equally between each of us; we have five each.* This can be modeled on page 3 of the Notebook file. Introduce the division symbol.

2. Read the problem on page 4 with students and ask them to suggest ways to solve it. After listening to their ideas, invite a student to share out the cabbages on screen, using division by sharing. Once the student has done this, use the Delete button to remove the red box to reveal the correct answer.

3. Explain the number sentence to students. Say: *We started with 14 cabbages. Then we shared them equally between two turtles, giving each turtle seven cabbages.*

4. Repeat this for the problem on page 5.

5. Read the questions on page 6. Ask students to choose a problem to solve and to write their answers on their individual whiteboards. Set the timer to 30 seconds and start it (click on the blue arrow).

6. Ask students to tell a partner their answer and explain how they worked it out. Address any misconceptions by working through both examples practically.

Independent Work

Give each student a copy of "Sharing" (p. 64). Ask students to figure out the answers to the problems (they may use counters). Encourage them to try writing a division number sentence for each problem.

Support less-confident learners by working alongside them to solve simple sharing problems practically. Challenge more-confident learners by asking them what to do with 7 ÷ 2. Talk about being able to halve the extra one, or leave a remainder of 1. Help students realize that the way they deal with the remainder depends on what is being shared.

Wrap-Up

Display page 7 of the Notebook file. Ask: *How many bananas can each monkey have?* Let students move the bananas to show the answer. Invite a volunteer to write the corresponding division calculation on the Notebook page.

Division as Grouping

* Represent repeated subtraction (grouping) as division.

Resources
* "Division as Grouping" Notebook file
* "Grouping" (p. 65)
* number line
* counters
* individual whiteboards and pens
* ball

Whiteboard tools
* Pen tray
* Select tool
* Delete button

Getting Started

Sit students in a circle with you in the center holding a ball. Tell them that they are going to practice counting backward in different steps. Give them a starting number and a step size. For example, say that you are going to start at 57 and count back by tens. Roll the ball to a student and ask the student to roll the ball back to you, stating the first number of the count (47). Roll the ball to another student; he or she must state the next number in the count (37). Continue this until 0 (or a number smaller than 10) has been reached.

Mini-Lesson

1. Go to page 2 of the "Division as Grouping" Notebook file. Explain division as making groups of equal amounts from a larger amount. Take 30 counters and stack them into groups of five. Say: *I have divided the counters into groups of five and there are six groups.* This can be modeled on page 2. Review the division symbol.

2. Read the problem on page 3 and ask students to suggest ways to solve it. Help them work out the answer using division by grouping. Invite a volunteer to come to the SMART Board to group the candies on-screen and to write in the answer. Then use the Delete tool to remove the red box to reveal the number sentence.

3. Explain the number sentence to students. Say: *We started with 12 candies, then we made groups of three candies until they had all been used, making four groups.* Show the calculation on a number line by starting on 12 and counting how many backward jumps of 3 it takes to get to 0.

4. Repeat this procedure for the problem on page 4.

5. Give out individual whiteboards and read the questions on page 5. Set the timer to 30 seconds and ask students to choose a problem to solve. Start the timer by clicking on the blue arrow. Check for any misconceptions.

Independent Work

Provide each student with a copy of "Grouping" (p. 65). Ask students to figure out the answers to the problems. Let them use counters, if necessary. Encourage students to try writing a division number sentence for each problem.

Support less-confident learners by working alongside them to solve simple grouping problems practically.

Wrap-Up

Go to page 6 of the Notebook file. Write a division number sentence and ask students to figure out the answer. Give students time to work with a partner to invent a problem that the number sentence shows. For example, 8 ÷ 2 = 4 could be: *A loaf of bread was cut into eight slices; sandwiches were made using two slices for each one. How many sandwiches were made altogether?*

Totals and Change

Getting Started

Discuss how to add together three numbers. Talk about the two main strategies—putting the largest number first and finding pairs that total a multiple of 10.

Open the "Totals and Change" Notebook file and go to page 2. The box contains two or three of each of these coin amounts: 1¢, 5¢, 10¢, 25¢, and 50¢. Ask a student to drag three numbers out of the box and write down the addition number sentence they create. Ask: *What is the answer? How did you figure it out?* Move on to four cards, if appropriate.

Mini-Lesson

1. Go to page 3 of the Notebook file. Ask students how they would figure out which coins they need to pay for something.

2. Give each pair of students a set of coins from pennies to dollars and ask them to put the coins in order from smallest to largest. Ask some volunteers to move the coins on page 4 to show their solution. Assess whether all coin values are known.

3. Give each pair a set of coins and show page 5. Ask each pair to make 29¢. Share the different ways that students find.

4. Next, ask each pair to make 29¢ using the least number of coins possible. Compare solutions and ask a student to drag the coins to display their solution on page 5.

5. Repeat this for 73¢ and 67¢.

6. Talk about how to add a group of coins together to find the total. Refer students back to the strategies used in Getting Started.

7. Finally, assess any students who seem confused by asking them to match the money boxes to the amounts on page 6.

Independent Work

Give each pair of students a set of "Find the Pairs" cards (p. 66) shuffled together. Review the rules for Concentration and explain that in the money version, students need to match the money totals with the coins. Encourage students to take their time figuring out the totals on each card. Create new cards with smaller or greater amounts to suit different abilities.

Wrap-Up

Give each pair of students a set of coins and specify an amount for each ability level. Challenge students to be the first to make their amount. Add an extra challenge by asking them to use the least number of coins possible. Ask: *What would happen if we couldn't make the exact amount? How do we work out what change we would need?* Write students' responses on page 7 of the Notebook file.

Shopping

Learning objective
- Represent information using $ and ¢ notation.

Resources
- "Shopping" Notebook file
- selection of coins
- selection of shopping items with sticky notes showing various prices
- calculators
- number lines
- individual whiteboards and pens
- printout of the receipt on page 7 of the "Shopping" Notebook file (one copy for each group of students)

Whiteboard tools
- Pen tray
- Select tool
- Delete button

Getting Started

Open the "Shopping" Notebook file and display page 2, which shows a partially hidden dime. Move the purple window around the coin and ask students to guess which coin is being shown. Write their suggestions around the box. How could they tell that it was a dime? Ask them how much they would have if they had ten of these coins. Consolidate students' knowledge that one hundred cents equals one dollar. Repeat with a dollar coin on page 3. Ask students to record this amount. Point out that there are two ways it can be recorded: 100¢ and $1.00. Ask what the .00 means.

Mini-Lesson

1. Look at the $ sign on page 4 of the Notebook file. Ask: *What does the symbol stand for?* Have students practice writing this symbol on their individual whiteboards and on the SMART Board.

2. Display page 5, which offers a shopping exercise. Drag two or three items out of the shopping basket and ask students to calculate the total cost of these items (using mental or informal strategies). Ask volunteers to present their answers on the SMART Board.

3. Write the total again on page 6 and invite students to decide which coins they need to pay for the items. Check the answers using the number line on page 5.

4. Ask students to read the answer in cents only, for example, one hundred and fourteen cents. Is there another way to say this? Demonstrate that 100¢ is the same as $1. Stress that 14¢ is 14¢. When the $ symbol is used, the ¢ is not, and the dollars and cents are separated by a decimal point.

5. Delete the items originally pulled from the box and repeat the activity. Ask children to first read the answer as cents and then as dollars and cents.

Independent Work

Divide the class into small groups and give each group a selection of objects with price labels on them. Invite them to estimate which items, when added together, will total 50¢ or more. Let them check their answers on a number line, carefully entering the amount. Encourage students to take turns reading the answer, first as dollars and cents, and then just cents. Ask students to find other items that total over 50¢ when added together. Ensure that students record their items and calculations, using the receipt template as shown on page 7 of the Notebook file. Challenge students to make four different amounts over $1 and $2. Simplify the activity by reducing the amount of money.

Wrap-Up

Ask pairs of students to complete the receipt on page 7 for specified prices. Invite them to demonstrate the strategies they used. Ask different children to use the number line to check the answers. Ask the whole class to read the final total as cents only and then as dollars and cents. Erase all the annotations and repeat if required.

Missing Numbers

Learning objective
- Calculate the value of an unknown in a number sentence.

Resources
- "Missing Numbers" Notebook file
- "What's Missing?" (p. 67)
- individual number lines
- colored pencils

Whiteboard tools
- Pen tray
- Select tool
- On-screen Keyboard

(Microsoft Excel is required to view the embedded spreadsheet in the Notebook file. Prior to opening the Excel file, ensure that your Excel security level is set to Medium [Tools menu > Macro submenu > Security command]. You will be prompted to enable or disable macros when you open the "Missing Numbers" Excel file; choose "Enable macros" for this file to work properly.)

Getting Started

Open page 2 of the "Missing Numbers" Notebook file. Press the thumbnail image to open the *Number Line Interactive Teaching Program*. Set the number line from 0 to 100 (click on the right or left arrows on the "min" and "max" icons) and place the markers on two numbers (click and drag on the circle below the number line to set the markers). Challenge students to work out the difference between the two numbers. Show the difference span to check the answer. Show the addition and subtraction equations (press on ? + ? = ?) and relate them to the numbers on the number line. Repeat this activity for different numbers.

Mini-Lesson

1. Go to page 3 of the Notebook file and press the button to open the Microsoft Excel file. Select the tab labeled "addition 2" at the bottom of the Excel spreadsheet. Use the up and down arrow buttons beneath the numbers or type in the numbers to create an equation, for example: 15 + ? = 23. (Use the On-screen Keyboard, accessed through the Pen tray or the SMART Board tools menu, to input numbers in the spreadsheet cells.)

2. Ask: *What do you need to do to figure out the missing number?* (Students need to calculate what must be added to 15 to make 23). Demonstrate this calculation on a number line—start on 15 and count the steps on to 23.

3. Next, choose the tab labeled "addition 3" and confirm that this type of missing number equation can be calculated in the same way as the previous one, because addition can be done in any order.

4. Then, choose the tab labeled "subtraction 2" and show that to calculate the missing number in an equation such as ? – 11 = 7, you need to calculate what number you start with if taking away 11 leaves 7. Demonstrate this calculation on a number line: To find the answer, start on 7 then add the 11 that were taken away back on.

5. Finally, choose the tab labeled "subtraction 3" and show that to calculate the missing number in a sum such as 24 – ? = 16, you need to calculate how many to take away from 24 to leave 16. Demonstrate this calculation on a number line: Start on 24 and count the steps back to 16.

6. You may wish to visit each type of problem in separate lessons initially.

Independent Work

Give each group a copy of "What's Missing?" (p. 67). Ask students to fill in the blanks, using a different color for the missing number. Give out number lines to enable students to check their answers.

Wrap-Up

Return to the Notebook file and use the *Number Line Interactive Teaching Program* on page 2 (with the addition or subtraction equation and the difference span showing) to work through some of the problems that students found tricky. Invite some of the more-confident learners to act as teacher and explain how to work out a problem to the rest of the class.

Odds & Evens

Learning objectives

- Describe patterns and relationships involving numbers or shapes.
- Recognize odd and even numbers.

Resources

- "Odds & Evens" Notebook file
- counters
- paper cups

Whiteboard tools

- Pen tray
- Select tool
- Area Capture tool
- Undo button

Getting Started

Review the definition of *odd* and *even* numbers. Remind students that even numbers can be shared into two equal groups, whereas odd numbers have an odd one left over. On page 2 of the "Odds & Evens" Notebook file, make two lists of the digits that are at the end of odd and even numbers.

Take students into a large space. Assign one end of the space as odd and the opposite end as even. Call out a number and tell students to move quickly to the correct end of the space.

Mini-Lesson

1. Share the problem on page 3 of the Notebook file with the class.

2. List all of the odd numbers up to 11 so that everyone is clear about what these are. State clearly that 0 is neither an odd nor an even number.

3. Display page 4 of the Notebook file. Ask one student to drag and drop the worms below the three birds so that one arrangement of the answer is displayed. Use the Area Capture tool to save the arrangement to the end of the Notebook file.

4. Check the arrangement as a class to ascertain that there are 11 worms altogether and that all the birds have an odd number of worms. Record the answer in the table on page 5, using page 4 as a reminder.

5. Go back to page 4. Use the Undo button to reset the page and ask another student to find a different arrangement. Record this new arrangement in the table on page 5. Repeat this until students believe that all of the arrangements have been found.

6. Ask: *How do we know all of the arrangements have been found?* Suggest that students could arrange the answers in the tables more systematically (such as: 1–1–9, 1–3–7, 1–5–5, and so on). Explain that this can help with checking to see if any arrangements have been missed out.

Independent Work

Show students the problem on page 6 of the Notebook file. Encourage them to try solving the problem in pairs, in the same way as the worm problem. Give students counters to represent the mice and paper cups to represent the cats. Challenge students to be systematic, as discussed in the whole-class shared work.

Supply less-confident learners with a copy of the table on page 8 of the Notebook file to help them record their findings.

Wrap-Up

Invite students to share the answers to their investigations. Talk about any differences in students' answers. Invite a student to move the mice on page 7. Work out a definitive set of answers as a class and invite a student to record it in the table on page 8.

Figure It Out

Learning objectives

- Identify and record the information or calculation needed to solve a puzzle or problem.
- Present solutions to puzzles and problems in an organized way.
- Explain decisions, methods, and results in spoken form, using mathematical language and number sentences.

Resources

- "Figure It Out" Notebook file
- "Work It Out" (p. 68)
- a set of cards with operations or phrases on them, such as: *shared by, plus, the difference between, groups of*

Whiteboard tools

- Pen tray
- Select tool
- Lines tool
- Highlighter pen
- Gallery

Getting Started

Open the "Figure It Out" Notebook file and go to page 2. Ask students to work in pairs to sort a set of cards with operation words or phrases on them (see Resources) into the type of operation they represent. Ask: *Are there any words or phrases that could represent more than one operation?* Talk as a class about how each pair sorted their cards. Explain that looking out for these words and phrases in word problems helps us to know which operation to use to figure out the answer. Ensure that students understand the terms *operation* (the type of problem) and *strategy* (a method for working out the answer). Write any notes or key words on page 2, if required.

Mini-Lesson

1. Go to page 3 of the Notebook file. Explain that Jo is a math detective who loves to solve math problems and wants students to help her.

2. Read the question on page 4 and ask a volunteer to come to the SMART Board and use the Lines tool to draw the hands on the clocks to show the two times in the question.

3. Ask: *What is the question asking us? What operation do we need to use and why? What strategies could we use to work out the answer?* Highlight any key words in the question (such as *7 o'clock, half past 9,* and *how long?*).

4. After modeling one strategy on the board, invite some children to share their strategies. Discuss their recording methods.

5. Repeat with the questions on pages 5 to 8. Encourage students to talk about their thinking. Remind them to check that they have actually answered the question being asked at the end.

6. Use tools from the Gallery such as on-screen teaching clocks, counters, and coins to help model questions. This is particularly useful for less-confident learners.

Independent Work

Put students in pairs of similar ability. Provide each pair with a copy of "Work It Out" (p. 68). Encourage the pairs to highlight the key words in each problem and discuss what is being asked. Tell them to show their strategies and the answers in the spaces provided. Supply a choice of tools for students to use, if required.

Ensure that less-confident learners are working within a comfortable range of numbers with which to do calculations. Talk further about different methods of recording with the more-confident learners.

Wrap-Up

Draw the class together throughout the lesson (as well as at the end) to talk about each question. Ask: *What was each question asking us? What operations did we need to use and why? What strategies did we use to work out the answer?* Use page 9 of the Notebook file to note key points, if required. Address any misconceptions and ask for alternative strategies where appropriate.

Money Problems

Learning objective
- Solve problems involving addition, subtraction, multiplication, or division using dollars and cents.

Resources
- "Money Problems" Notebook file
- "How Much Money?" (p. 69)
- purses containing different amounts of money (one for each child)
- highlighters
- pencils
- items for a role-play store (see Wrap-Up)

Whiteboard tools
- Pen tray
- Select tool
- Highlighter pen

Getting Started
Give each student a purse of money and ask them to figure out the total amount of money in the purse. Tell students to swap purses with a friend to check their answers.

Mini-Lesson
1. Open the "Money Problems" Notebook file and go to page 2. Look at the symbols (+ – x ÷) and review what each of them represents.

2. Read the problem on page 3 of the Notebook file and talk with students about what the question is asking and what operation they will need to use. Highlight any key words that help identify the operation needed.

3. Drag the pictures and symbols into the white box to illustrate the problem. For example, attach the 15¢ label to the apple. Make duplicate copies of the pictures and symbols if they are needed by selecting the Clone option from an object's drop-down menu.

4. Ask: *What strategy could we use to figure out this answer?* Discuss different ways to solve the problem as a class.

5. Look at pages 4 and 5 in the same way, talking about the operation needed and the strategies that could be used to figure out the answer.

6. As an assessment, ask students to work in similar-ability pairs to solve the problems on page 6. Share the answers as a class, talking about which operations were needed and which strategies worked well.

Independent Work
Pair up students with similar abilities. Provide each pair with a copy of "How Much Money?" (p. 69). Encourage the pairs to highlight the key words in each problem and discuss what is being asked. Ask students to record the problem and answer as a number sentence. Encourage the use of pictures and writing to aid understanding.

Ensure that less-confident learners are working within the range of numbers that they can comfortably calculate with. Challenge more-confident learners by asking them to work with amounts of money over $1.

Wrap-Up
Set up a pretend store and ask students to invent questions surrounding the role-play for their peers to answer (for example, *One pencil costs 30¢. How much do 3 pencils cost?*). Discuss what information, operations, and strategies will be needed to solve each problem. Encourage students who answer the questions to act out their solutions using the store role-play equipment.

Word Problems

Learning objective
- Solve one- and two-step problems involving numbers, choosing and carrying out appropriate calculations.

Resources
- "Word Problems" Notebook file
- counters or interlocking cubes
- digital camera or scanning equipment

Whiteboard tools
- Pen tray
- Select tool

Getting Started

Ask a group of children to demonstrate how to role-play a real-life scenario but to represent the problem in writing. For example:

There are 3 swings in the playground and 18 children in our class. How many need to line up behind each swing so an equal number of children uses each swing?

Write the problem on page 2 of the "Word Problems" Notebook file. Encourage the group to represent the swings with a chair, for example, and to divide students one at a time to stand behind it. Ask: *How many children are lined up behind each swing?* Return students to their seats and ask them how they would write the answer to the word problem in a sentence. Emphasize that the problem was carried out using a division/sharing method.

Mini-Lesson

1. Read the text on page 3 of the Notebook file and look at the picture of the tractor and trailer. (Children are generally more motivated to solve a word problem when it is illustrated.)

2. Ask students to imagine the context. Ask: *Have you ever visited a farm or gone on a tractor ride? If so, can you remember how many children rode on the trailer?*

Independent Work

Ask students to work in pairs to figure out how many trips the tractor trailer needs to make to give every child a ride. The emphasis here is not on recognizing key words, but on understanding the context and, with it, imagining the scenario. They will be using their own experience to answer the question. Students may not recognize the type of calculation needed immediately. They may use role-play, illustrations, notes, or representations using manipulatives, such as counters.

Use page 4 of the Notebook file with less-confident learners to help them visualize the problem. Demonstrate with a smaller number of children if necessary. (Fifty figures are provided on-screen but delete the number as appropriate.) Move four children into the trailer. Drag the tractor and trailer around the farm to the finish line and then move students out of the trailer. Stop after ten minutes and share initial responses.

Wrap-Up

During the course of the mini-lesson, scan in or photograph with a digital camera different initial responses, and display them on-screen. Ask the pairs who made the responses to share how they thought about the problem. Conclude with the reasoning behind the answer.

On page 5 of the Notebook file, demonstrate by using repeated subtraction along a number line that 50 divided by 4 equals 12 with a remainder of 2. Discuss what this remainder means. Ask: *Will the two children miss a tractor ride?* Discuss what would happen and conclude that the tractor would have to make an extra trip around the farm (a total of 13). Write this answer in a sentence underneath the initial question on page 3 of the Notebook file.

Sort the Aliens

Learning objective

- Use Venn diagrams or tables to sort data and objects using more than one criterion.

Resources

- "Sort the Aliens" Notebook file
- set of classroom objects/shapes to sort
- sorting circles or large paper with two circles drawn on it
- labels

Whiteboard tools

- Pen tray
- Select tool
- On-screen Keyboard
- Undo button

Getting Started

Open the "Sort the Aliens" Notebook file and go to page 2. Look at the aliens that have been placed around the page. Ask students to discuss, in pairs, how they would sort this group using one criterion (such as color, number of legs, and so on). Select one pair's suggestion. Write the criterion in the sorting label, then drag the relevant aliens into the sorting circle. State that the aliens outside the circle do not fit the data set, but they too could be labeled. Create a label for these aliens.

Mini-Lesson

1. Go to page 3 of the Notebook file. This shows the same aliens, but this time there are two sorting circles.

2. Ask students how they could sort the aliens into the two circles. Choose different criteria from the one used in the Getting Started activity. Decide on the two criteria together. Label the circles by double-clicking Set 1 and changing the text to your new sorting label. Do the same for Set 2.

3. Ask whether all the objects can be sorted into these two circles and if there are aliens that match both criteria. One example where one alien will meet both criteria is "green aliens" and "two eyes."

4. Discuss how to present objects if both criteria are met. Demonstrate how the circles can overlap. Introduce this sorting format as a *Venn diagram*.

5. Invite students to the SMART Board to sort the objects into the circles. Pose questions such as: *How has this object been sorted? Why has it been placed there?*

6. Use the Undo button until the page is reset and experiment with different criteria to explore the ways in which the aliens can be sorted. For example, "yellow aliens" and "aliens with four legs," or "green aliens" and "yellow aliens."

Independent Work

Invite students to classify and then sort a series of objects (pencils, shapes, and so on) according to one criterion. Have them write a label on the sorting circle. Repeat the activity for two criteria, challenging students to present the sorted objects in a Venn diagram.

Allow groups of students to take turns sorting the aliens on page 3 of the Notebook file. Have students add their own labels to the sorting circles. They can either convert handwritten words to text by pressing the Right Mouse button and selecting the Recognize option or they can add text using the On-screen Keyboard.

Wrap-Up

Go to page 4 of the Notebook file to assess whether students understand how to sort using a Venn diagram. Ask groups of students to think about how the objects have been sorted and what the circle labels could be. Annotate their suggestions. For example, one label could be "aliens with three eyes" and the other "aliens with two mouths."

Telling Time

Learning objectives
- Use units of time (seconds, minutes, hours, days) and know the relationships between them.
- Read the time to the quarter hour.

Resources
- "Telling Time" Notebook file
- "The Time Is…" (p. 70)
- large teaching clock
- balls or other equipment for timed activity (see Getting Started)
- individual whiteboards and pens

Whiteboard tools
- Pen tray
- Select tool

Getting Started

Open the "Telling Time" Notebook file and go to page 2. Ask students to close their eyes when you say "go" and open them again when they think one minute has passed. Start the on-screen timer and share one minute with students, so that they know how long it actually is.

Next, ask them to estimate how many times they can do an activity, such as bounce a ball, in one minute. Test these estimates by carrying out the activity. Record the results on the Notebook page.

Mini-Lesson

1. Use a large teaching clock that displays both analog and digital to show some times. Go to page 3 of the Notebook file, which shows an analog and digital clock.

2. Ask: *What time does the clock read?* Review the function of the hour and minute hands and how these relate to the numbers on a digital clock. To rotate the clock hands, select one and then press and drag the arrow end of the line. Use a Pen from the Pen tray to write the corresponding time on the digital clock.

3. Practice reading *o'clock, half-past, quarter-past,* and *quarter-to* times. Ensure that both analog and digital displays are used and compared.

4. Open the quiz on page 4. Ask students to write their answers on their individual whiteboards before inviting a volunteer to press the button next to the answer that he or she thinks is correct. Repeat this for all six questions.

5. Using the clock on page 5, demonstrate how to work out times that are earlier or later than a given time. Show the hands moving around the clock and ensure that all students understand that quarter of an hour equates to a quarter turn of the minute hand.

6. Do the second quiz, on page 6, in the same way as the one on page 4.

Independent Work

Give each student an enlarged copy of "The Time Is…" (p. 70). Encourage students to read the times and write them down in words on the line beneath each clock. Supply a word bank of the time and number words they may need.

Less-confident learners will need to practice reading only *o'clock* and *half-past* times to begin with. As an extension, ask students to revisit each clock and work out the challenges beneath each one.

Wrap-Up

Investigate students' work to see whether most of their difficulties were with telling the time or with passage of time. Ask students to display given times and to display times that are later or earlier than a given time. Encourage students to talk about how they worked out the answer. Use this session to assess students' progress. Use page 7 of the Notebook file to compile a summary of what students have learned.

What Time Is It?

Learning objective
- Read the time on a 12-hour digital clock and to the nearest five minutes on an analog clock.

Resources
- "What Time Is It?" Notebook file
- "At What Time?" (p. 71)
- individual whiteboards and pens
- paper
- pencils
- scissors
- glue

Whiteboard tools
- Pen tray
- Select tool

Getting Started

Open the "What Time Is It?" Notebook file and establish the learning objective with students: They will be learning about telling the time with analog and digital clocks. Go to page 2. Ask students to say and then record the time on their individual whiteboards. Establish that the time is 4 o'clock.

Draw attention to the digital clock next to the analog clock. Again, ask students to say and then record the time on their whiteboard. Establish that the two clocks show the same time. Ask students to compare and contrast how the times appear.

Repeat with the times on pages 3 and 4. Page 3 shows the times to the half hour and quarter past on both the analog and the digital clocks, and page 4 shows the time at quarter to the hour and at five minutes to the hour.

Mini-Lesson

1. Ask students to discuss, in pairs, what time they do certain activities, such as getting up, eating breakfast, leaving for school, and arriving at school.

2. Go to page 5 of the Notebook file and open the "What time is it?" activity. This sequencing program shows different images of morning routines. Ask the pairs to order the images according to their experiences. There may be discussions about whether the face should be washed before the teeth are cleaned or vice versa.

3. Drag the agreed first image into the first space (top left), then continue to sequence the other pictures according to the opinions of the majority of the class. (Although there is an "Am I correct?" button that takes one particular sequence as correct, students' own routines may vary.)

4. Once the sequence is agreed, ask students what time is displayed on the analog clock in the first image of the sequencing activity. Ask: *How would this be written on the digital clock?*

5. Drag the digital clock template from the right to the first image and write the correct time on it.

6. Repeat with another picture (using the digital and analog clock templates) until all six images have a time written in both formats.

Independent Work

Hand out copies of "At What Time?" (p. 71). Ask students to cut out and sequence nighttime routines, according to their own experiences. After the pictures have been cut out and glued into the correct order, ask students to record an approximate time for each event in both analog and digital formats. Simplify the activity by asking students to sort the pictures to given times on the hour and half hour, from 5 to 7 P.M., and/or use the analog clock only.

Wrap-Up

Invite students to share their sequenced pictures. Ask: *Do you go to bed at different times or about the same time? Who has dinner at half-past five?* Invite students to think about important times in their school day. Make a list of all of these times on page 6 of the Notebook file. Recognize which activities happen in the morning or afternoon and whether they use A.M. or P.M.

What Do I Use to Measure?

Learning objectives

- Know the relationships between kilometers and meters, meters and centimeters, kilograms and grams, liters and milliliters.
- Choose and use appropriate units to estimate, measure, and record measurements.

Resources

- "What Do I Use to Measure?" Notebook file
- "Measurements" (p. 72)
- set of measuring tools, one per table (ruler, meter stick, tape measure, measuring cups, and weights/scales)

Whiteboard tools

- Pen tray
- Select tool
- On-screen Keyboard

Getting Started

Discuss the objective for this lesson as shown on page 1 of the "What Do I Use to Measure?" Notebook file. Discuss which is larger or smaller: kilometer, meter, centimeter, or millimeter? Ask students which measurement would be used for each of the questions shown on page 2. Drag the correct word to answer each question. Discuss the range of responses, as well as the reasons why some measurements have not been chosen.

Mini-Lesson

1. Reiterate what is actually being measured when you are talking about length (how long/tall something is); weight (how heavy something is); and volume (how much liquid something will contain).

2. Look at the images of different measuring tools on page 3 of the Notebook file and provide each table with a set of measuring tools. Select and drag the correct labels for each tool (bearing in mind what each item measures and the units it measures in).

3. Prompt students with questions such as: *What tool would you use to measure the height of a tree/the amount of juice left/the weight of a car?* Let students discuss the answer as a group, then invite one student from each table to come to the SMART Board and draw a circle around the correct image.

4. Often the understanding of a kilometer is difficult for students to grasp. Use opportunities such as walking to the playground or library to discuss what walking a kilometer actually feels like.

Independent Work

In order to estimate, students need to have knowledge of the maximum measurement displayed on measuring tools. Ask them to look at the tools on their table and to record the maximum measurement from the scales. Hand out copies of "Measurements" (p. 72) to each group. Ask the group to identify suitable units of measurement (in the "What we are measuring" column) and to estimate measurements for objects within the school or classroom. For example, the height of the door, the distance around the playground, the amount a paint jar holds, and so on. Have the group record estimates in the table on the reproducible sheet.

Wrap-Up

Ask each group to present their estimates. Use the range of answers as a teaching point to look at how to find out which estimate is nearest. Establish that the estimate for the classroom door is over one meter. Discuss how to measure the length of a door if you only had one meter stick. Ask: *What strategies could you use?* Demonstrate how to use a meter stick to measure the door. Complete the table on page 4 of the Notebook file with students using the results from their Independent Work.

Favorite Fruits and Drinks

Learning objectives

- Answer a question by collecting and recording data in lists and tables.
- Represent the data as pictograms to show results.

Resources

- "Favorite Fruits and Drinks" Notebook file
- "Favorite Drinks" (p. 73)
- a selection of fruits
- 8-1/2" x 11" paper
- colored pencils
- glue

Whiteboard tools

- Pen tray
- Select tool
- Area Capture tool

Getting Started

Ask students to sort themselves in a variety of ways (such as length of first name, age, and shoe size). Ask questions about how they are sorted. For example: *How many letters does the longest name have? How many people have size 3 shoes?* Suggest grouping students to make it easier to count them.

Mini-Lesson

1. Go to page 2 of the "Favorite Fruits and Drinks" Notebook file. Read the question at the top of the page. Explain that you would like the class to investigate this. Then open the linked "Favorite Fruits" pictogram by pressing the thumbnail image on the screen.

2. Give students an opportunity to taste some fruit. (**Safety note:** Check for any food allergies beforehand.) Ask them to consider which of the fruits they like best.

3. Ask: *How can we find out which fruit our class likes the most?* Take suggestions from students and give constructive feedback about their ideas.

4. Explain that the information can be used to create a pictogram. Ensure that everyone understands what a pictogram is and how it works.

5. Invite each student to place their vote for their favorite fruit on the pictogram displayed on the screen. Keep stopping to ask questions, for example: *Which fruit is most popular now? Are there any fruits that nobody likes? How many children like apples best?*

6. When the pictogram is complete, use the Area Capture tool to take a snapshot of it. Place the image beneath the original question on page 2. Write the answer underneath the pictogram and save the page.

Independent Work

Open page 3 of the Notebook file and read the question at the top. Explain that students are going to investigate this in pairs. List six suggestions of favorite drinks in the space provided, then ask students to vote for their favorite by raising their hand. Record the number of votes next to each drink. Supply each pair with a plain sheet of paper, a copy of "Favorite Drinks" (p. 73), colored pencils, and glue. Ask students to create a pictogram to show the answer to their investigation. Suggest using one glass to represent one student and coloring each type of drink a different color.

Challenge more-confident learners to use one glass to represent two children (so a glass will need to be cut in half to deal with an odd number of votes).

Wrap-Up

Encourage students to add titles and labels to their work. Ask them to make sure that they have answered the question. Scan in some of students' work on page 4 of the Notebook file and evaluate its effectiveness in communicating the answer. (Upload scanned images of students' work by selecting Insert, then Picture File, and browsing to where you have saved the images.) Ask other questions about the data to assess students' understanding.

Animals Pictogram

Learning objectives
- Answer a question by collecting, organizing, and interpreting data.
- Use pictograms to represent results.

Resources
- "Animals Pictogram" Notebook file
- "Animals" (p. 74)
- plain or graphing paper
- pencils

Whiteboard tools
- Pen tray
- Select tool
- Capture tool
- Page Sorter
- On-screen Keyboard

Getting Started

Open the "Animals Pictogram" Notebook file and start the pictogram activity on page 2. Point out the animals at the side of the pictogram. Ask general questions about the animals, such as: *Is your favorite animal here? Do you have one of these animals as a pet?* Ask children why this data might have been collected (for example, to see which animals students like).

Tell students that for this lesson, they will be using the pictogram to look at which animals students like the most. Ask students what the title should be and where you should write it.

Mini-Lesson

1. Encourage suggestions as to what the title of this pictogram could be. Type the agreed title in the box provided, using the On-screen Keyboard.

2. Tell students that when the pictogram is completed, they can use the results to find out which animals the class likes best and least.

3. Demonstrate how to build up the pictogram by dragging and dropping a picture from the grid into a column. Each animal has its own column; you can't put one type of animal in another's column. To remove a picture, simply drag it off the grid.

4. Invite each student to come to the SMART Board to select their favorite animal.

Independent Work

Have students create their own animals pictogram. They can choose a different question, such as: *Which animal would you like to see in a zoo?* Show students how to create their own pictogram chart on graphing paper, reminding them to draw the two axes and to include a title. Ask students to cut out the animals on their copy of "Animals" (p. 74) and glue them onto the squares in the chart. Let students make up their own results for others to interpret. Suggest that pairs swap completed pictograms and interpret the new pictogram, recording answers to a series of questions written on the board. For example:

- *What is this pictogram about?*
- *Which animal has the most pictures? How many?*
- *Which has the least? How many?*
- *Were some animals not used at all? Why do you think this is?*

Wrap-Up

Keep the pictogram on-screen and press the "Start again" button to reset the pictogram. Ask a student to complete the pictogram on screen, using his or her own data. Take a snapshot of the completed pictogram using the Capture tool and drag it to page 3 of the Notebook file via the Page Sorter. Alternatively, copy the snapshot, press the back button, and paste it onto page 3. Ask each group to propose a question about the pictogram to another group, for example, *What was the most popular animal visited at a zoo?* Display page 4 to see an example of how different pictograms can be created on a Notebook page.

Colors Bar Chart

Getting Started

Show the completed bar chart and pictogram on page 2 of the "Colors Bar Chart" Notebook file. Ask students to identify similarities and differences between the two charts, for example, that both have numbers on the vertical axis. Explore more challenging questions such as the difference in sample size. List these on page 3.

Mini-Lesson

1. Go to page 4 of the Notebook file. This shows a table with the column headings, "Colored pencil supply" and "Number of pencils." Tell students that they will be transferring this information to a bar chart.

2. Open the "Colors bar chart" activity. Discuss what the labels on the vertical and horizontal axes mean.

3. All of the columns are set to 1. Increase and reduce the number by dragging the top of the column up or down to line up with the numbers. Set the columns to 0.

4. Ask students to read aloud the first color and number from the table. Demonstrate how to represent this number in a bar chart. Repeat with the rest of the colors.

5. Interpret the finished bar chart together. Students may conclude that one color is popular because it has a large representation on the bar chart, or that the most popular is the one that has the least representation because it gets used up quickly!

Independent Work

Divide the class into small groups. Ask each group to sort a mixture of colored pencils by colors. They should first record the number of each color in a table and then transfer the information onto a copy of "Bar Chart" (p. 75). Show them how to draw the table and fill in the bar chart. They should color the bars using the correct color. Pose questions on page 6 to encourage students to interpret their data. For example: *How many red pens were there? What is the difference between the number of white and black pencils? Of which color are there fewest?*

Wrap-Up

Ask each group to report back on their findings. Reset the bar chart by pressing the "Start again" button and use students' figures to complete the bar chart on the board. If the number of pencils exceeds ten, annotate the top of the column with *+1* to signify 11, *+2* for 12, and so on. Pose the same questions as before and encourage students to interpret this data. Use the Area Capture tool to take a picture of the completed bar chart and add it to page 6 via the Page Sorter. Ask the groups to discuss who in the school would find this information useful (such as the teacher that reorders art materials). Page 7 gives an example of how a bar chart can be created on a Notebook page if you opt to use different colors or wish to change the scale.

Shape Names

Learning objective
- Visualize common 2D shapes and 3D solids.

Resources
- "Shape Names" Notebook file
- "Find the Shapes" (p. 76)
- cards with pictures of 3D shapes (see Before You Start)
- a selection of 3D shapes (see Before You Start)
- colored pencils

Whiteboard tools
- Pen tray
- Select tool
- Shapes tool
- Highlighter pen

Before You Start

Prepare a set of cards, each with a picture of a different 3D shape on it, such as a cube, rectangular prism, cylinder, cone, and so on. Also collect a selection of 3D shapes (or a variety of packaging boxes) that correspond to the pictures on your cards.

Getting Started

Divide the class into two groups according to ability. Give the less-confident half of the class a solid 3D shape and ask them to describe it to a partner. Give the more-confident half of the class a prepared card (see Before You Start) and ask them to describe the shape drawn on it to a partner. If necessary, write words on page 2 of the "Shape Names" Notebook file to help students in their descriptions. Explain to students that each of the cards can be matched to a solid 3D shape. Ask them to find their new partners by matching the cards to the shapes. Use the Shapes tool to add shapes to page 2, if required.

Mini-Lesson

1. Look at the 2D shapes on page 3 of the Notebook file. Ensure that students can read all of the shape names. Ask: *Do you know any of the names of these shapes?* Invite students to match the shape names to the shapes.

2. Give a description for each shape as they are labeled, to help reinforce students' knowledge. For example: *A triangle always has three corners and three straight sides.*

3. Repeat the activity for 3D shapes on page 4. If possible, supply solid 3D shapes for students to handle, as they may find it difficult to visualize a drawn 3D shape.

4. Show page 5 of the Notebook file and challenge students to find the listed shapes in the picture. Emphasize the difference between a square and a cube (this is a common misconception when they are drawn). Highlight the shapes as found, if required.

Independent Work

Give each student a copy of "Find the Shapes" (p. 76). Ask students to find how many of each shape are in the picture. Tell students to mark or color the shapes once they have counted them, to avoid repetition. Encourage them to compare answers regularly with a partner.

Wrap-Up

Ask a student to choose a shape from a range of 2D and 3D shapes. Encourage the rest of the students to ask yes/no questions to determine the identity of the chosen shape. For example: *Does it have any square faces?* By the process of elimination, students can work out which shape is the chosen shape. If required, use page 5 of the Notebook file to display the chosen shape and to discuss its properties. Be strict about the use of accurate terminology and correct shape names during the game.

Shape Sorting

Learning objective
- Sort, make, and describe shapes, referring to their properties.

Resources
- "Shape Sorting" Notebook file
- a selection of 2D and 3D shapes
- prepared Venn diagrams, tables, and shapes to cut out (see Independent Work)

Whiteboard tools
- Pen tray
- Select tool

Getting Started

Divide the class into small groups. Put a selection of 2D and 3D shapes on each group's table and ask students to spend one minute, as a group, discussing the shapes and their properties. Explain to them what faces, edges, and corners are.

Choose a mystery shape and give students clues to identify that shape. For example: *This shape has 12 edges.* Encourage them to discard the shapes they know it cannot be after every clue and ask them to explain how they eliminated these shapes. Consider adding key words to page 2 of the "Shape Sorting" Notebook file.

Mini-Lesson

1. Go to page 3 of the Notebook file and confirm with students that a pentagon is any shape with five straight sides and five corners, while a hexagon is any shape with six straight sides and six corners.

2. Sort the shapes, using the drag-and-drop method. Count the sides each time to check.

3. Move on to page 4. Ask students to describe and name some of the shapes they can see. Explain that the overlapping part of the Venn diagram allows for shapes to be a member of both sets (those with both curved and straight edges). Sort the shapes together.

4. Look at page 5 and explain how to use the table. Ask students to determine what shape properties each section of the table can contain. Sort the shapes together.

Independent Work

Give students a Venn diagram with two overlapping sets. Label one set "3D shapes" and the other set "curved edges." Supply students with a range of 2D and 3D shape pictures and ask them to sort these into the correct places on the diagram.

Give less-confident learners a Venn diagram with two separate sets and ask them to sort two shapes that they find it difficult to distinguish between, such as cubes and rectangular prisms. Provide actual shapes rather than pictures for any 3D shape sorting. Challenge more-confident learners with a table. Label the top "pyramid" and "not a pyramid." Label the side "square base" and "not a square base." Ask students to sort 3D shapes. Once completed, ask them to comment on the shapes that have ended up together. Working in pairs will stimulate conversation about the properties of the shapes.

Wrap-Up

Put shapes into bags and ask students to feel and then describe them to the class so that they can try to guess what they are. Make a note of good shape vocabulary on page 6 of the Notebook file. Sort the revealed shapes into a large Venn diagram, created with hoops or ropes on the classroom floor.

Shapes and Patterns

Learning objectives
- Relate 2D shapes to drawings of them.
- Describe, visualize, classify, draw, and make the shapes.

Resources
- "Shapes and Patterns" Notebook file
- "Shapes and Patterns" (p. 77), copied onto cardstock and cut apart (or a selection of 2D shapes)
- paper
- pencils
- individual whiteboards and pens

Whiteboard tools
- Pen tray
- Select tool
- Highlighter pen
- Shapes tool
- Delete button

Getting Started

Look at the sequence of shapes on page 2 of the "Shapes and Patterns" Notebook file. Ask students to predict what the next shape in the sequence might be. Discuss why this is difficult to predict at this stage. Move the box to reveal the shape. Uncover a smaller version of the sequence at the bottom of the page, then ask students to describe verbally the sequence for the next four places. (There is an infinite number of these shapes on the page, so they can be dragged to continue the sequence.)

Working in pairs and with students using individual whiteboards, have one person choose two shapes and start a pattern. After the fifth shape in the pattern, ask the partner to predict what the next shape will be and to draw the pattern for the next five places.

Mini-Lesson

1. Go to page 3 of the Notebook file. Tell students that a shape is hidden in the dark. Move the flashlight around to see it. Ask students to guess what the shape is. Move slowly around the edges of the shape and encourage students to count the sides.

2. Ask those who predicted correctly to say how they could tell it was an octagon. Write the octagon's properties around the shape.

3. Go to page 4 and build up a pattern around the hexagon. Insert a square using the Shapes tool and position it against a flat edge of the hexagon using the rotate function (click on the shape and drag around the green circle). The square may need to be resized to fit (click on the shape and drag on a corner).

4. Repeat with seven additional squares. Establish the properties of a square. Ask: *Are the squares positioned at an angle still squares?*

5. Ask students to identify the shape that would fit the gaps between the squares. This could be a triangle, rhombus, or parallelogram. Add one of these shapes and resize, rotate, and drag it to fit between the squares.

6. Decide whether to tessellate the image (explain that *tessellate* means to arrange or make a pattern of a shape without gaps or overlapping) or to create a pattern containing gaps.

Independent Work

Give students copies of the cut-apart "Shapes and Patterns" (p. 77) to create a vertical or horizontal pattern using three different shapes. Ask students to record the pattern on paper. They may use a different color for specific shapes. Some may be able to develop this by filling a whole page. Less-confident learners may find it easier to use one or two shapes.

Wrap-Up

Look at the images on page 5 of the Notebook file. Focus on one of the images and, using a Highlighter pen, trace around the shape that is repeated. Ask students to list the properties of that shape and to decide whether this shape can tessellate. Annotate the image with their suggestions. Repeat this with the rest of the images. Finish the lesson by creating an example of a repeating pattern using the Shapes tool on page 6 and agreeing on a definition of the term *tessellation* on page 7.

Position

Learning objective
- Follow and give instructions involving position.

Resources
- "Position" Notebook file
- "Position Island" (p. 78)
- individual whiteboards and pens

Whiteboard tools
- Pen tray
- Select tool

Getting Started
Open page 2 of the "Position" Notebook file. Explain to students that you will be asking them addition and subtraction questions that they can compute mentally. Invite them to share the answers and strategies used to work them out. Then ask a student to write the answer in a defined place on the grid. For example, say: *Write the answer two spaces below the circle.*

Mini-Lesson
1. Use page 3 of the Notebook file to introduce the objective.

2. In pairs, give students one minute to make a list on their individual whiteboards of as many position phrases as possible (such as *beneath* and *far away from*). Share these ideas as a class and define the meaning of any less-obvious phrases.

3. Go to page 4 and ask students to name the objects on the grid.

4. Point to the star in the pink square. Ask students to tell a partner the position of the star in two different ways, for example: *The star is next to [or to the right of] the frog* and *The star is two squares above the strawberry.* Write students' position vocabulary in the box on the right-hand side of the page.

5. Repeat until the location of all the stars has been identified.

Independent Work
Put students in pairs and give each student an enlarged copy of "Position Island" (p. 78). Out of view of their partners, ask each student to design their own island in the top map grid by placing five things on it, such as a haunted castle or a golden chicken's nest. Ensure that each item is drawn in only one square on the grid. Ask students to take turns describing to their partners what they have added to their own island and the position they have put it in. The student listening must draw their partner's described island on the bottom map grid in the position their partner described. Encourage students to compare their maps at the end and discuss any errors made.

Less-confident learners will need adult support to scaffold their language and to ensure that they remain on task without getting frustrated.

Wrap-Up
Ask a student to choose an object in the classroom and describe where it is, so that other students can guess what it is. Explain that they must be precise if they want other students to be able to identify the object that they have chosen. Encourage the use of more adventurous language to describe the position of the object. Use page 5 of the Notebook file to record the description.

Moving Along a Route

Learning objective
- Follow and give instructions involving position, direction, and movement.

Resources
- "Moving Along a Route" Notebook file
- "Robot Directions" (p. 79)
- counters
- pencils
- simple maze marked out on floor (see Wrap-Up)

Whiteboard tools
- Pen tray
- Select tool

Getting Started

Take students into a large space. Demonstrate what a quarter turn is and describe this as a *right-angled turn*. Show students which way is clockwise and counterclockwise. Ask them questions such as: *If you make three quarter turns clockwise and then two quarter turns counterclockwise, which way will you be facing?* Try out the instructions to test students' answers.

Mini-Lesson

1. Open the "Moving Along a Route" Notebook file and use page 2 to introduce the commands needed to make a rabbit move around the screen. Invite students to come to the SMART Board and move the rabbit on the grid in the various directions. Explain that they are not completing the maze at this stage.

2. Ensure that all students are confident in their use of left and right.

3. Go to page 3 and give students a few minutes to describe to a partner the route the rabbit will need to take to the end of the maze. Point out the key words: *up, down, left,* and *right*. Write the first instruction in the first box, *Up 6*, to get the discussion started. Invite students to write the subsequent instructions in the boxes provided.

4. Once they have done this, use the Eraser from the Pen tray to rub over the blue boxes to reveal the hidden instructions. Invite a volunteer to come to the SMART Board to move the rabbit according to the instructions.

5. Move on to page 4, which shows a ladybug on a grid. This ladybug moves in a different way from the rabbit. Instead of moving forward and sideways to go around corners, this ladybug needs to turn on the spot and travel in the direction that it is facing. It can only make quarter turns. Invite students to move and turn the ladybug.

6. Look at page 5 and work as a class to determine the route that the ladybug will need to take to the end of the maze. Invite students to drag and drop the required instructions and then to move the ladybug.

Independent Work

Give each student a copy of "Robot Directions" (p. 79) and a counter. Ask each student to find a route for the robot (counter) through the maze and draw it with a pencil. Ask students to write the instructions that the robot must follow on the lines beneath the maze.

Support less-confident learners by writing their directions for them or allowing them to record their directions orally using a tape recorder. Challenge more-confident learners by giving them a robot that can only move forward and make quarter turns. Draw an arrow on the counter to support students in recalling in which direction the robot is traveling. Suggest that they move the counter along the route as they write their instructions.

Wrap-Up

Mark out a simple maze on the playground or hall floor. Put students in pairs and assign one student in each pair as the robot and the other as the controller. Blindfold the robot and ask the controller to lead the robot through the simple route by giving clear directional instructions. Ensure that there are no tripping hazards nearby. Assess each student's ability to give and understand instructions during this activity.

Spot the Right Angle

Learning objectives

- Identify right angles in 2D shapes.
- Compare angles with a right angle.

Resources

- "Spot the Right Angle" Notebook file
- 2 strips of cardboard fastened together by a brad, for each pair of students (or use geostrips)
- printed or magazine pictures
- colored pens
- paper

Whiteboard tools

- Pen tray
- Select tool
- Pen tool
- Area Capture tool
- Blank Page button
- Page Sorter

Getting Started

Ask pairs of students to use two strips of cardboard with a brass fastener to discuss and make right angles. Ask questions to reinforce the definition of a *right angle* (the point at which the vertical and horizontal lines meet). State that we use the term *acute* and *obtuse* for angles smaller or larger, respectively, than a right angle. Look at and discuss the different angles on page 2 of the "Spot the Right Angle" Notebook file.

Mini-Lesson

1. Look at page 3 of the Notebook file. Ask the pairs to identify three right angles in the picture, using their right-angle templates to justify their findings.

2. Use the right-angle shape, which has already been placed on the page, to confirm students' answers, rotating the shape by pressing it and dragging the green dot, if necessary.

3. Select a red Pen to draw over the right angles. Students may mistake obtuse and acute angles as right angles. Discuss the differences between obtuse (more than 90°) and acute (less than 90°) angles and highlight the obtuse angles in yellow and acute ones in blue.

4. On angles that require further clarification, use the Area Capture tool to take a snapshot of the relevant section of the image, paste this onto a blank page, and then enlarge it to look at the image in more detail.

5. Repeat this process for the images on pages 4 to 7.

Independent Work

Using the right-angle template, identify right angles from a printed or magazine picture. Challenge students to find five right, five obtuse, and five acute angles. Encourage them to record their findings by: drawing over the angle with the colors used during the Mini-Lesson; cutting out the image and positioning it in a table with headings for the three different types of angles; or drawing the objects, and highlighting and labeling the angles.

To challenge more-confident learners, discuss that angles are measured in degrees, and allow pupils to investigate what a protractor might be used for.

Wrap-Up

A number of angles are hidden behind circles on page 8 of the Notebook file. Reduce the size of a circle to gradually reveal a small section and ask pupils to state whether the angle is right, acute, or obtuse. Ask whether they have enough information or whether they need more to be revealed. Reveal the whole angle by reducing or deleting the circle. *What kind of angle is it?* Drag the black box over the angle to reveal whether it is an obtuse, acute, or right angle. Repeat this, if necessary, with more of the hidden angles. Review the definition of a right angle on page 8.

Reflections

Learning objectives
- Draw and complete shapes with reflective symmetry.
- Draw the reflection of a shape in a mirror line along one side.

Resources
- "Reflections" Notebook file
- safety mirrors
- scissors
- colored paper

Whiteboard tools
- Pen tray
- Pen tool
- Select tool

Getting Started
Load the "Reflections" Notebook file and display the learning objectives on page 1. Ask pairs of children to stand and face each other. One student should stand in a position that has a line of symmetry, for example, arms straight out to the front, touching at fingertips. The other student must copy that position and stand alongside their partner. Stress that the position should be mirrored in the same way as in a real mirror. Go to page 2 and discuss what the terms *mirror line* and *reflection* mean.

Mini-Lesson
1. Open page 3 of the Notebook file, which shows an arrow with a mirror line on the *y*-axis. Ask students what this arrow would look like if it were reflected in a mirror that was placed along the vertical line.

2. Clone the arrow and position the second arrow alongside the first. Ask students if this is what they see in the mirror. If students are unsure, place a large teaching mirror along the line on the SMART Board or ask them to sketch the arrow and use individual mirrors to work it out.

3. Delete the incorrect reflection and invite a student to draw the correct position of the arrow.

4. Press the Right Mouse button and set the background to a different color to reveal the reflection.

5. Repeat this on page 4 and ask what the single arrow would look like if it were reflected in a horizontal line. Ask a student to draw the new reflection. Set the background to a different color to reveal the correct reflection.

Independent Work
Ask students to write their name in block capital letters on one side of a folded piece of colored paper. Make sure they leave some space between their letters and the fold line. Have students cut out the letters, leaving the folded edge intact. Then have them unfold the paper to reveal the name reflected along one line of symmetry. Ask students to work out how they could produce their name so that it is reflected in two lines of symmetry. Let them experiment with new paper. The easiest way is to place two sheets together and repeat the first step; when opened up, place the two sheets alongside each other. Support those students with fine-motor-skills difficulties by providing precut letters reflected in one line of symmetry.

Wrap-Up
Ask students to share their work by displaying it at the front of the class. Ask them if any letters look the same when reflected. Go to page 5 of the Notebook file. Ask students to record what they think the first letter is and share answers. Reveal the letter and discuss how it could have been an *F* or an *E*. Identify the line of symmetry. Ask the class to identify the second hidden letter (*G*). If there is time, consider which letters do or do not have lines of symmetry.

Lines of Symmetry

Learning objectives
- Draw and complete shapes with reflective symmetry.
- Draw the reflection of a shape in a line of symmetry along one side.

Resources
- "Lines of Symmetry" Notebook file
- mirrors with straight edges
- sets of everyday objects
- rulers
- paper
- scissors

Whiteboard tools
- Pen tray
- Select tool
- Undo button
- Delete button

Getting Started

Open the "Lines of Symmetry" Notebook file and go to page 2. Give each student a piece of paper and ask them to fold it in half. Ask them to cut a shape in the piece of paper, keeping the fold intact. When they fold out the paper, they will see that the shape on one side will be the mirror image of the other side. Use a mirror to test whether this is correct.

Ask students to fold a new sheet of paper in a different way, or to fold it twice. Tell them to cut out a different shape and open it out to show what they have reflected. Review the terms *mirror line* and *reflection* from the previous lesson ("Reflections," p. 49).

Mini-Lesson

1. Go to page 3 of the Notebook file. Invite a student to draw the other half of the shield (its reflection).

2. Move the box to reveal the hidden half of the shield. Establish that the shield is symmetrical. Demonstrate this by holding a mirror to the line where the image is exactly reflected, then draw that line in red along the mirror edge.

3. Cover half of the shield and cut that shape out of a folded piece of paper. Unfold it and compare it to the shape on the board. Point out that the fold line is the line of symmetry.

4. Ask students to find the lines of symmetry in their cutout shapes from the Getting Started activity (above).

Independent Work

Divide the class into small groups and give each group a set of everyday objects. If the object is 3D, state that for the purposes of this activity, students will need to choose one side of the object to look at. Using a mirror, ask students to investigate whether the different objects have one or more lines of symmetry. They should then sketch the object and indicate the symmetry line using a ruler and a red pencil. If an object has no lines of symmetry, students should draw it and write this fact underneath.

In the meantime, small groups can take turns at the SMART Board. Using page 4 of the Notebook file, invite students to draw the missing halves of the objects, deleting or moving the boxes to see if they are correct. Invite them to add the line of symmetry using the Pen tool and a real ruler laid on the SMART Board. Identify if there is more than one line of symmetry or even none. Press the Undo button until the page is reset and start the activity again for new groups.

Wrap-Up

Ask students to share what they have learned about lines of symmetry in their investigation. *Which objects have more than one or no lines of symmetry?* Challenge students to look for and make a list of examples of objects with one or more lines of symmetry on their way home.

Fill in the Numbers

What's missing? Fill in the blanks.

1.　　4　　5　　6　　7　　8　　9　　___　　11

2.　　18　　28　　___　　48　　58　　68　　78　　88

3.　　63　　53　　43　　33　　___　　13　　3

4.　　86　　87　　88　　___　　90　　91　　92　　93

5.　　21　　31　　___　　51　　61　　71　　81

6.　　___　　93　　92　　91　　___　　89　　88　　87

7.　　72　　___　　52　　___　　32　　22　　12

8.　　35　　36　　37　　___　　39　　40　　___　　42

9.　　___　　57　　56　　55　　54　　___　　52　　51

10.　　47　　___　　49　　50　　___　　52　　53　　54

Math Lessons for the SMART Board: Grades 2–3 © 2011, Scholastic

Arrow Number Cards

0 1 2 3 4 5

6 7 8 9 10

20 30 40 50

60 70 80 90

Math Lessons for the SMART Board: Grades 2–3 © 2011, Scholastic

Hundreds, Tens, and Ones

100	200	300
400	500	600
700	800	900

10	20	30	40
50	60	70	80

90	1	2	3	4	5

6	7	8	9

Four in a Row

- You will need: counters in two different colors (one color for each player).

INSTRUCTIONS

- Take turns on the spinner. Find two numbers on the board that can be either added or subtracted to make the number on the spinner and use the counters to cover them both. The first player to get four counters in a row (horizontally, vertically, or diagonally) wins the game.

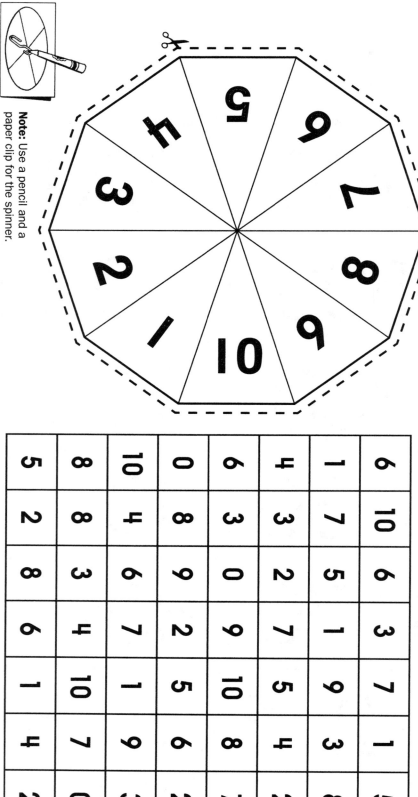

Note: Use a pencil and a paper clip for the spinner.

6	10	6	3	7	1	5	4
1	7	5	1	9	3	8	9
4	3	2	7	5	4	2	0
6	3	0	9	10	8	7	10
0	8	9	2	5	6	2	5
10	4	6	7	1	9	3	10
8	8	3	4	10	7	0	9
5	2	8	6	1	4	2	1

Fact Cards

8 + 6	12 – 3	4 + 3	6 – 2
9 + 9	15 – 8	7 + 6	10 – 2
5 + 4	18 – 12	13 + 2	14 – 7
12 + 8	20 – 6	15 + 3	20 – 8
16 + 4	17 – 9	8 + 8	13 – 5

Number Triplets

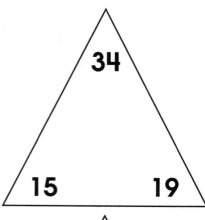

34

15   19

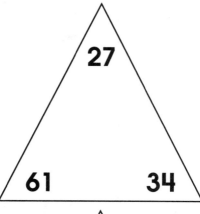

27

61   34

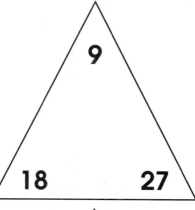

9

18   27

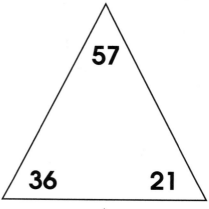

57

36   21

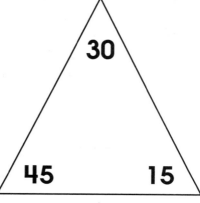

30

45   15

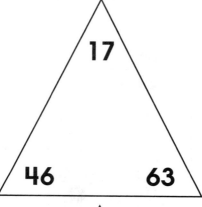

17

46   63

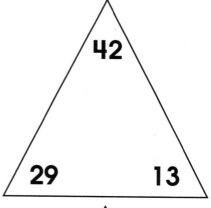

42

29   13

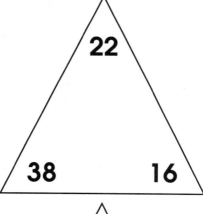

22

38   16

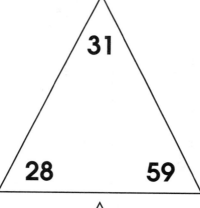

31

28   59

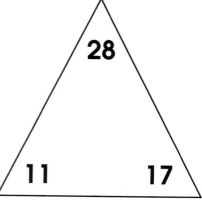

28

11   17

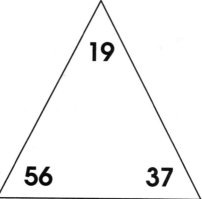

19

56   37

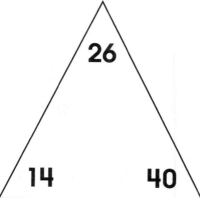

26

14   40

Ladybug Flip Flap

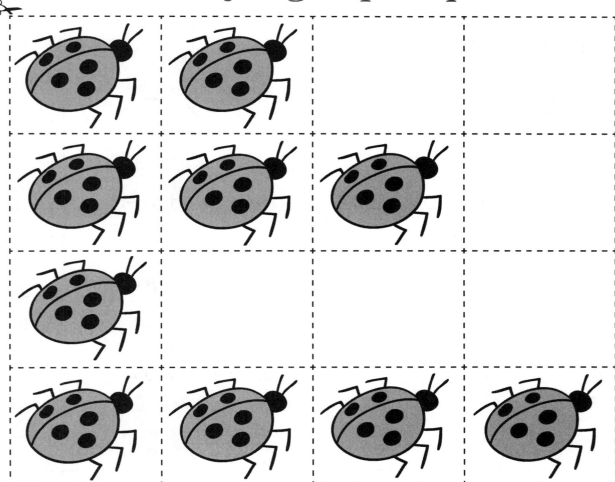

Instructions for how to make a flip flap.

1. Cut out each square above individually.

2. Stick the 16 individual cards facedown onto a sheet of clear sticky-backed plastic. Arrange the cards in the order they are displayed above. Leave a small, even gap (about 2 or 3mm) on all sides between each card.

3. Stick clear, sticky-backed plastic over the top of the cards so that the cards are encased between the two layers. Trim the edges to neaten it.

4. Fold the 'flip flap' along each of the gaps between the cards to establish a crease.

Math Lessons for the SMART Board: Grades 2–3 © 2011, Scholastic

Adding on to 10

Add and find the sums.

1. $2 + 5 + 8 =$ _____

2. $7 + 1 + 2 =$ _____

3. $6 + 9 + 4 =$ _____

4. $8 + 3 + 7 =$ _____

5. $2 + 9 + 3 =$ _____

6. $9 + 1 + 6 =$ _____

7. $5 + 5 + 2 =$ _____

8. $4 + 4 + 6 =$ _____

9. $8 + 2 + 7 =$ _____

10. $2 + 9 + 5 =$ _____

11. $1 + 2 + 8 =$ _____

12. $5 + 6 + 5 =$ _____

13. $4 + 7 + 8 =$ _____

14. $6 + 3 + 6 =$ _____

15. $7 + 3 + 3 =$ _____

Math Lessons for the SMART Board: Grades 2–3 © 2011, Scholastic

Making Easy 10s

1. $6 + 7 =$ _____

2. $8 + 4 =$ _____

3. $5 + 9 =$ _____

4. $7 + 8 =$ _____

5. $9 + 7 =$ _____

6. $3 + 9 =$ _____

7. $6 + 8 =$ _____

8. $8 + 9 =$ _____

9. $7 + 4 =$ _____

10. $4 + 9 =$ _____

11. $15 + 8 =$ _____

12. $13 + 9 =$ _____

13. $6 + 18 =$ _____

14. $9 + 12 =$ _____

15. $14 + 9 =$ _____

16. $18 + 4 =$ _____

17. $7 + 19 =$ _____

18. $17 + 8 =$ _____

19. $16 + 5 =$ _____

20. $19 + 8 =$ _____

Multiply by Adding

2 x 4	2 x 6	2 x 7	2 x 3
5 x 3	5 x 5	5 x 4	5 x 7
10 x 4	10 x 2	10 x 8	10 x 6
2 x 8	2 x 5	2 x 9	5 x 6
5 x 8	10 x 7	10 x 5	10 x 9

Multiplication Bingo Question Cards

2 x 1	2 x 2	10 x 1	10 x 2
2 x 3	2 x 4	10 x 3	10 x 4
2 x 5	2 x 6	10 x 5	10 x 6
2 x 7	2 x 8	10 x 7	10 x 8
2 x 9	2 x 10	10 x 9	10 x 10

Name _____ **Date** _____

Teacher: Prepare bingo cards by filling in the grids with multiples of 2 and 10.

Multiplication Bingo

- -

Multiplication Bingo

Math Lessons for the SMART Board: Grades 2–3 © 2011, Scholastic

Multiples of 2, 5, and 10

Some of these numbers are multiples of 2, 5, or 10.
Can you sort them?

345	72	380	990
546	14	7	44
523	999	87	85
26	18	25	74
675	300	340	388
102	395	546	1,000

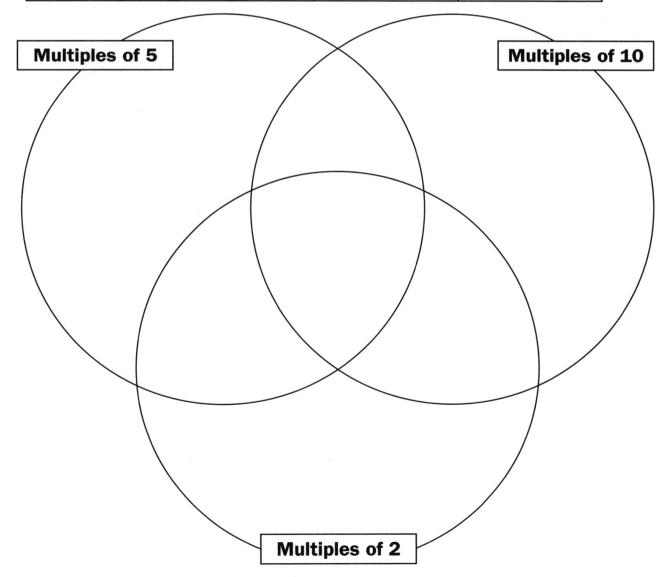

Multiples of 5   **Multiples of 10**

Multiples of 2

Sharing

1. Two children shared 8 candies. How many candies did each get?

_____

2. Ten dogs shared 50 treats. How many treats did each dog get?

_____

3. A piece of rope measures 18 inches. If it is cut into 2 equal pieces, how long would each piece be?

_____

4. If 20 stickers are shared among 5 boys, how many stickers will each boy get?

_____

5. A bag of seed holds 10 ounces. If the bag is shared between 5 birds, how much seed can each bird have?

_____

6. Jan's mom made 20 cupcakes for Jan's party. Ten children were at the party; how many cupcakes did each child have?

_____

7. A mother bird has 5 babies. How many worms can each eat if the mother bird collects 30 worms altogether?

_____

8. Tom cooked 6 sausages. He shared the sausages with Jill. How many sausages did they each have?

_____

Quick Finisher

Work out the answer to these division problems.

$15 \div 5 =$ _____ $12 \div 2 =$ _____ $60 \div 10 =$ _____

$18 \div 2 =$ _____ $40 \div 10 =$ _____ $25 \div 5 =$ _____

Math Lessons for the SMART Board: Grades 2–3 © 2011, Scholastic

Grouping

1. How many groups of 2 children can be made from a class of 20 children?

_____

2. How many bags of 10 apples can be made from a box of 60 apples?

_____

3. How many 5¢ jellybeans can be bought with 25¢?

_____

4. How many 2-foot ropes can be made from a 14-foot rope?

_____

5. How many 10-ounce bags of chocolates can be made from a 50-ounce box of chocolates?

_____

6. How many 2-liter bottles of water can be filled from an 18-liter barrel?

_____

7. How many strips of 5 stamps can be made from a strip of 45 stamps?

_____

8. How many 5-player football teams can be made from a group of 30 children?

_____

Quick Finisher

Work out the answer to these division problems.

$35 \div 5 =$ _____ $14 \div 2 =$ _____ $50 \div 10 =$ _____

$12 \div 2 =$ _____ $90 \div 10 =$ _____ $40 \div 5 =$ _____

Find the Pairs

80¢	43¢	28¢	64¢	32¢
25¢	16¢	37¢	42¢	65¢
36¢	74¢	49¢	30¢	51¢

Math Lessons for the SMART Board: Grades 2–3 © 2011, Scholastic

What's Missing?

$16 + \underline{} = 25$	$64 - \underline{} = 51$	$\underline{} + 29 = 40$	$\underline{} - 15 = 15$
$\underline{} - 18 = 4$	$13 + \underline{} = 27$	$67 - \underline{} = 61$	$16 + \underline{} = 30$
$17 + \underline{} = 30$	$\underline{} - 8 = 19$	$13 + \underline{} = 21$	$76 - \underline{} = 42$
$22 - \underline{} = 12$	$4 + \underline{} = 42$	$\underline{} - 20 = 72$	$\underline{} + 67 = 75$
$\underline{} + 23 = 36$	$45 - \underline{} = 38$	$52 + \underline{} = 65$	$96 - \underline{} = 89$

Work It Out

Jon bought an apple for 32¢ and a bottle of water for 49¢. He paid for his shopping with $1.

How much change did he get?

Jon, Mel, Des, Gav, and Shaz have 2 rabbits each. Each rabbit eats 5 carrots a day.

How many carrots is that altogether?

Anna had 57 stickers in her collection. She bought 13 more stickers, then gave 9 stickers to her friend.

How many stickers does Anna have now?

Kendra had a bag of 24 jellybeans. She shared the jellybeans equally with her best friend, Sal.

How many jellybeans did Sal have?

Math Lessons for the SMART Board: Grades 2–3 © 2011, Scholastic

How Much Money?

Kat bought 3 apples and 4 bananas. Each apple cost 5¢ and each banana cost 10¢.

How much did the apples and bananas cost altogether?

Tim had 37¢. He spent 24¢ on a comic book, and then his grandmother gave him 15¢.

How much money has Tim got now?

Mom made $18 at a yard sale.
She shared the money equally with Kay and Dom.

How much money did Mom, Kay, and Dom each get?

Lucy bought a pen for 48¢ and an eraser for 26¢.
She paid for them with a $1 bill.

How much money did Lucy have left over?

Name _____ **Date** _____

The Time Is...

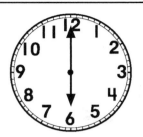

The time is

_____

What time will it
be in 3 hours?

_____

The time is

_____

What time will it
be in 5 hours?

_____

The time is

_____

What time was it 2
hours ago?

_____

The time is

_____

What time was it 6
hours ago?

_____

The time is

_____

What time will it
be in 4 hours?

_____

The time is

_____

What time was it 7
hours ago?

_____

The time is

_____

What time will it be
in half an hour?

_____

The time is

_____

What time will it be
in half an hour?

_____

The time is

_____

What time was it
half an hour ago?

_____

The time is

_____

What time was it
one and a half
hours ago?

_____

The time is

_____

What time was it a
quarter of an hour
ago?

_____

The time is

_____

What time will it be
in a quarter of an
hour?

_____

At What Time?

Cut out the pictures and put them in order. Then write in the times.

Measurements

Object	What we are measuring	What do we use to measure this?	What we think the measurement will be	The actual measurement

Favorite Drinks

Animals

Cut out these animals to create your own animals pictogram. If you'd like, use the blank squares to draw a different animal.

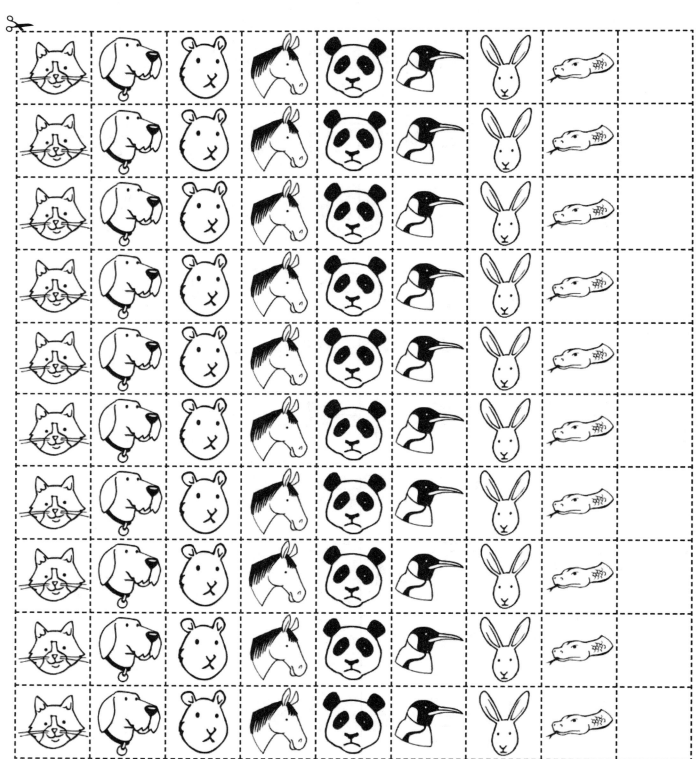

Bar Chart

Find the Shapes

Shape name	Number found
Cone	
Rectangular prism	
Cylinder	
Pyramid	
Sphere	
Hexagon	
Circle	
Square	
Rectangle	

Shapes and Patterns

Cut out these shapes. Use them to make patterns.

Position Island

My island

My partner's island

Robot Directions

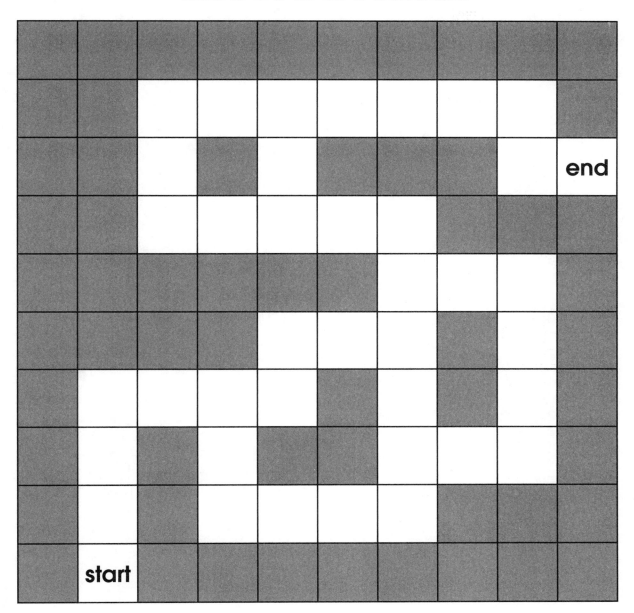

Instructions

_____

_____

_____

_____

_____

Notes

Math Lessons for the SMART Board: Grades 2–3 © 2011, Scholastic